THE
FORTUNE-TELLER'S
I CHING

THE
FORTUNE-TELLER'S
I CHING

Kwok Man Ho, Martin Palmer
and Joanne O'Brien

Ballantine Books · New York

*This book is dedicated
to our parents and
grandparents*

Library of Congress Catalog Card Number: 86-48009

ISBN: 0-345-34539-8

Cover design by Richard Aquan
Manufactured in the United States of America
First American Edition: August 1987
10 9 8 7 6 5 4 3 2 1

Contents

Preface

There are few if any who would dispute that the *I Ching* is now accepted worldwide as a classic of religious literature. To be sure, though many use it, few people understand it – which is after all the fate of most religious or ideological classics, be they the *I Ching,* the Bible or *Das Capital.* Yet it has not always been accepted as a classic; and in looking at how the West now views the *I Ching* it is important to see how attitudes have changed over the last hundred years. For our edition we went to the Chinese of today who use this book daily because we felt the need to provide a new translation and totally new kind of commentary.

The danger with any religious text which comes to us from another and very different culture is that we are not able to approach it without bringing our own values to bear upon it. So a historian approaching the New Testament asks of it questions which, while interesting in their own right, are not the kind of questions which a Christian believer asks of it. Both are valid within their own worlds, but the claim to greater significance must surely lie with the believer who is the latest in the line of believers and who is thus part of a continuing interpretative tradition which can be traced back to the faith which was its source, the very reason for the book's existence. It is as a mixture of historians and believers that we have approached our task. Two of us come from the West, and although we are familiar with much in Chinese language and culture, we are not of that language and culture. Therefore we bring to the task different questions from those of our Chinese colleagues at the International Consultancy on Religion, Education and Culture (ICOREC), for whom the *I Ching* is part of their birthright. They are the heirs to the continuing tradition of how to use and interpret the book and one of them has studied and used it for over twenty years in his role as a diviner and Buddhist initiate. We hope that in this new translation we can be the bridge by which our Chinese colleagues are able to pass to the Western reader a more complete and contemporary understanding of a truly remarkable book.

The *I Ching* has only been available to the West in

translation since 1834. At first it attracted virtually no attention at all, being such a difficult book to 'read'. It was also felt to lack the sort of straightforward ethical and humanistic qualities which are found in, say, *The Analects* of Confucius or the *Book of Mo Tzu,* and which so appealed to Enlightenment man. While the West, in the aftermath of the American and French revolutions, was willing to look for other models of practical ethical government, it was not yet ready to look for other religious insights. Thus both the *I Ching* and the *Tao Te Ching* had to await a change in thinking and attitudes before they could begin to make their mark.

Acknowledgements

We wish to express our grateful thanks, first, to our colleagues in ICOREC, especially Barbara Cousins, Pallavi Mavani, Kerry Brown, Liz Breuilly and Li Fung Shi. We also wish to thank our families and friends, Chinese and Western, at home and in the Far East, who helped us to make sense of all the material. Finally, to our editors, Oliver Caldecott and Sue Hogg, thank you for your patience and care and for being so demanding.

1
What Is the *I Ching*?

什麼是易経？

The *I Ching* is one of the world's oldest books. Quite how old it is or, possibly, how old the material within it is we are unlikely ever to know with any great accuracy. Its roots, like all things of any significance in China, lie back in the dim mists of prehistory and are the province of legend and semi-history. Perhaps it is fairest to allow the *I Ching* itself to tell its side of the story first, as recorded in 'The Great Commentary', the 'Ta Chuan', which forms one of the appendixes to the main text. In the section 'Hsi Tz'u' comes this description of the discovery and significance of the *I Ching*.

When in ancient times Fu Hsi ruled the world, he looked up to observe the phenomena of the heavens, and gazed down to observe the contours of the earth. He observed the markings of birds and beasts and how they were adapted to their habitats. Some ideas he took from his own body, and went beyond this to take other ideas from other things. Thus he invented the eight trigrams in order to comprehend the virtues of spiritual beings and represent the conditions of all things of creation. He knotted cords and made nets for hunting and fishing. This idea he probably adopted from the hexagram *Li*.

After Fu Hsi died Shen Nung arose. He carved a piece of wood into a plowshare and bent another piece to make a handle, and taught the world the advantages of plowing and weeding. This idea he probably took from the hexagram *I*. He set up markets at midday and caused the people of the world to bring all their goods and exchange them and then return home so that everything found its proper place. This he probably took from the hexagram *Shih-ho*.

After Shen Nung died, the Yellow Emperor, Yao, and Shun arose. They comprehended change and caused the people to be unwearied, transforming them with spirit so that they were rightly ordered. When the Changes has run one course to its extreme, then it changes, and by changing it is able to continue, and by continuing it achieves longevity. Thus the Changes receives help from Heaven: good fortune and nothing that is not beneficial.

The Yellow Emperor, Yao, and Shun allowed their upper and lower garments to hang down and the world was ordered. This they probably took from the hexagrams *Ch'ien* and *K'un*.

They hollowed out logs to make boats and shaved pieces of wood for rudders, and by the advantages of boats and rudders opened up new roads of communication to distant places for the profit of the world. This they probably took from the hexagram *Huan*.[1]

Needless to say, the author of this text, who is supposed to be Confucius, had a very high opinion of the *I Ching*. According to all ancient Chinese authorities, the origins of the *I Ching* lie with Fu Hsi. Fu Hsi is the primordial bringer of the gifts of civilization to the world or, more precisely to the Chinese. He is credited with having invented the Chinese calendar,[2] marriage, writing, the civil administrative system and many other essentials of civilized life. However, it is for his discovery of the eight trigrams that he is held in greatest reverence in China. Virtually all paintings of Fu Hsi show him holding the eight trigrams. Quite what these are we shall come to shortly.

Fu Hsi is called the August One, and he was the first such person. After him came two more August Ones, of whom Shen Nung was the third and last. He is credited with the discovery of agriculture, hence his use of the hexagram *I* to make the plough.

After the Three August Ones came the Five August Emperors, of whom the Yellow Emperor, Yao and Shun are three. They likewise are seen as having laid the foundation stones of how Chinese society should organize itself and by what principles.

By citing these great founding fathers of civilization, the writer of the 'Hsi Tz'u' was showing how the *I Ching* was part of that very process and thus gave it the sort of pedigree which was essential if it was to hold its place as the foremost divination system in China. Whether or not we are inclined to believe that Fu Hsi, some time around 3000 BCE, existed and actually discovered the eight trigrams, what we are faced with in the *I Ching* is a system which goes back well beyond 1100 BCE and which may indeed have its roots in greater antiquity. However, there is little more that can be said about its likely date of origin as a system, and we must therefore turn our attention to its development and growth, catching glimpses of it as it moves into recorded history, and perhaps from them come to understand a little more of what it actually is.

So far as we can tell, the *I Ching* originally consisted of the sixty-four hexagrams which are derived from the original eight trigrams. A trigram is a block of three parallel straight lines, each line being either complete (unbroken) or broken. By using all the possible permutations of these two types of line in a set of three, the eight trigrams are arrived at (see p. 42).

In one version of his legend, Fu Hsi says that he first saw the eight trigrams marked out on the shell of a turtle. This is a very significant comment because it gives us the first real clue to the possible origin of this entire system. Until 1977 this particular legend seemed unintelligible or, at the very least, of no historical significance. But then came a report from mainland China that, during investigations of a Chou-dynasty site (c. 1028–221 BCE) near Ch'i-shan, turtle shells had been found which had not only been used for divination purposes, a practice which was known, but which had been inscribed with crude characters or signs. It had been known for many years that the Shang (1523–1028 BCE) and the Chou dynasties had used turtle shells for recording official transactions, but here was the first evidence of their use both for divination and for recording the messages received in divination.[3]

How did the Shang and Chou people use these turtle shells for divination and how might this have led to the discovery of the trigrams? The answer actually lies buried in the Classic *The Book of Poetry*, the *Shih Ching*. In the section 'Greater Odes of the Kingdom' there is a poem which describes how the ruler T'an Fu led his people to found a new settlement on the plains of Chou, reputedly during the year 1325 BCE.[4] The way in which they chose the site for their new home is described thus:

> The plain of Chou looked so rich and beautiful,
> Its celery and sowthistle as good as dumplings.
> Here we will start, here we will seek advice.
> Here mark our turtle shell.
> It says, 'Stop', it says, 'This is the time'.
> This is where we shall build our homes.
>
> [Our translation]

The turtle or tortoise shells were used for divination as follows: a small dent or a hole was made in the shell and heat, perhaps from a smouldering stick, was applied until the shell cracked. The lines which were formed by these cracks were then 'read' – and here is the origin of the earliest forms of Chinese characters. At the same time it is very likely that here also is the origin of the trigrams, for on many of the turtle shells used for divination series of inscribed lines, often three in number, are to be seen. Perhaps we have here verification of at least part of the legend of Fu Hsi and the turtle shell.

Whatever the truth of this, the eight trigrams were soon combined into the sixty-four hexagrams. This was done by simply putting the trigrams in pairs in all the possible combinations: thus the sixty-four hexagrams came into being. Yet when, where, why or how this happened we have no idea. All that we know is that at some stage, possibly in the late Shang or the early Chou dynasty, the sixty-four hexagrams were in existence.

Here the mists of time still firmly shroud the progress of the book. We know from various records such as the *Chou Li* (*The Record of Rites of the Chou*) that there used to exist three divination books, the first called *Lien Shan*, the second *Kuei Tsang* and the third *Chou I* – the precursor of the current *I Ching*. What these books were or how they were used is hard to tell, especially as, barring a few fragments, the first two books have disappeared, while the *Chou I* has undergone many transformations. Yet judging from accounts in the *Li Chi* (*The Record of Rites*, one of the five Classics), the use of tortoise shells was a major element in the rituals of divination derived from the legend of Fu Hsi and the eight trigrams.[5] But yet again we are in uncertain territory. The texts mentioned above are of unknown date, and even if they do seem to point fairly clearly to a series of books on divination whose origins involved the use of tortoise shells, we cannot say more than this. Nor can we do more than guess that these books and the sixty-four hexagrams were in existence before 1000 BCE in some form or another.

King Wen

We now come to another story about the *I Ching*. This concerns the second major figure in its traditional history, King Wen. He is credited with having written the brief descriptions or judgements which accompany each of the hexagrams. The story tells how King Wen (*c.* 1160 BCE), the ruler of a small state, was captured by the invading forces of the Shang dynasty. He spent only a year in gaol before being released, and while in prison he made good use of his time by writing the descriptions of the hexagrams. This seems to indicate that until that time the hexagrams had been used on their own, subject to the interpretive skills of individual diviners.

It is worth pausing here to consider these descriptions or judgements. Undoubtedly they are very early, though again, unless we feel inclined to accept at face value the story of King Wen, we cannot give them an exact date. Perhaps we are best settling with Hellmut Wilhelm, that 'modern Chinese research, which for a long time held widely divergent views as to the time of origin of the *I*

Ching, has now come back to placing this stratum of text in the time of King Wen.'[6]

But what are these judgements? Where do they come from or, if we wish to accept King Wen's authorship, from where did he derive them? This is one of the most perplexing aspects of the *I Ching*. Quite frankly, to many people these judgements seem virtually incomprehensible. This is partly due to the nature of ancient Chinese, which uses language in a very different way from us. For instance, many of the judgements consist of only a few characters. There are no pronouns, no tenses, no plurals or singulars. There are often simply verbs or nouns standing on their own or with another verb or noun. It is up to each interpreter or translator of the ancient Chinese text to bring to it certain assumptions of grammar and construction in order to make a relatively coherent sentence out of it. Yet even when that has been done we are left with a series of bald statements which seem to have little in common except their terseness and ambiguity. In the earliest encounters of the West with these texts, their cryptic nature led commentators to see them either as statements of great profundity precisely because they were so incomprehensible, or as crude statements of a rather basic or demotic nature to be regarded as a collection of dislocated peasant sayings. Something of this divide continues to this day and has even come to affect the way certain Western-trained Chinese approach the material.

Yet there is a continuous tradition which has so far been overlooked by earlier Western writers on the *I Ching* and which we believe can cast at least a little light on these statements and their particular style. The tradition of divination did not stop with the *I Ching*. Indeed, as we shall see, the ancient methods, such as the casting of sticks, which were used with the *I Ching* have been passed on to other areas of divination. And in current Chinese communities throughout the world there are to be found books containing statements which are very similar in their style to the judgements of the hexagrams. Each book is associated with a particular deity, who is believed to have written down divinatory messages while a human being. We shall later examine the divination method used, but for the moment let us look at a couple of modern divinatory messages such as those you would receive at temples like Wong Tai Sin in Hong Kong or Kuan Yin in Singapore.

Lot 7. Your way ahead is blocked and barred. The streams are bearing earth and clay. If you explore in foreign places, you'll find no work, no home to rest. [Kuan Yin][7]

Lot 80. While drinking with his friends he was alarmed because in his cup a small snake he found. In truth it was but the shadow of a hung-up bow. Fear leads nowhere, for good luck will come through. [Wong Tai Sin][8]

It could always be argued that these predictions, which, just like those of the *I Ching*, require further explanation, have been modelled on the *I Ching*. Yet we prefer to think that we are witnessing here an unbroken tradition of Chinese predictions and divinations: quite simply, this is the style in which such predictions or judgements have always been given, and they have to be seen and judged in that light. What is perhaps of interest is that these systems have usually originated in peasant cults such as that found around Wong Tai Sin, and here we may have a glimpse of the origins of the *I Ching*'s style of judgements.

One further point needs to be made. The more cryptic a statement, the more scope there is for the professional who can interpret it. In the past, works on the *I Ching* have been remarkable for the way they ignore the social, economic and political factors out of which the book arose and through which it has passed. Let us not forget that these judgements have always needed, so far as the Chinese are concerned, a professional to interpret them fully. Similarly the predictions of Wong Tai Sin, Kuan Yin and others of more recent date also require professionals who make their living from telling you what they really mean. Possibly their style owes something at least to those who have made a living from such divination! For instance, why did King Wen get out of prison so easily? Maybe he used his knowledge of the hexagrams to ensure his release? There must have been some reason behind writing them down. After all, Westerners have a story in their Scriptures about a man who used divination skills to be released from prison – Joseph and the dreams of Pharaoh (Genesis, 39–41).

To recapitulate, according to legend, by about 1150 BCE the sixty-four hexagrams and their brief judgements had been created. It is at this point that the story of the *I Ching* takes a sudden leap forward.

Legend tells how Tan, the Duke of Chou and the son of King Wen, won back his father's lands from the Shang dynasty and established the family line of Chou which led to the Chou dynasty itself. King Tan added that most distinctive aspect of the *I Ching* as we have it now, the commentaries on the individual lines of each hexagram. Here again we encounter the same cryptic Chinese style as in the lines attributed to King Wen. If anything, Tan's commentaries are even more complex and at times appear downright odd. Yet if we look at the Chinese predictive writings of today which are outlined above, we can see that Tan's lines also fit this pattern. And they certainly provide yet more ground for the professional diviner and philosopher who thinks that he can interpret them. Again, who can say whether King Tan really did write these lines? All that is of importance is that from now on the book had a singular format and this is reflected in the fact that it was known for many hundreds of years as the *Chou I - The Changes of Chou*.

Confucius and after

We now come to the sixth to fifth centuries BCE, for attached to the main text of the *I Ching* is a further series of commentaries and appendixes often called the 'Ten Wings'. These are attributed to the great sage of China, K'ung Fu-tzu, commonly Latinized to Confucius. Born in 551 BCE, he died in 479 BCE. The core of his teachings harks back to the moral order of the past – as he saw it. This was captured in his idea of filial loyalty which upheld the strict hierarchical order of the Chinese system of government. Although he was little appreciated during his lifetime, he came to exercise a vast power over the very structure and norms of later Chinese society right up to our own time. Yet the nature of his links with the *I Ching* presents a number of problems. Traditionally he is credited with the major commentaries and appendixes, but whether he actually wrote them is quite another matter. From what we know of K'ung Fu-tzu, there are aspects of his life which indicate that he might have been interested, and aspects which seem to show he would not have been involved with such a book. On the positive side, we know that he venerated all things to do with the past. He revered the works of the ancient rulers and sought in his writings and teaching to return the people of his own time to the standards which he found spelt out within these ancient records. Thus it is likely that he would have been interested in a book of such undisputed antiquity as the *I Ching*, especially one with such royal associations. However, it is also the case that his interest in the spiritual or divinational world seems to have been very limited. There is the famous exchange between K'ung and his follower Chi-lu as recorded in *The Analects*, XI,12.

Chi-lu asked how the spirits of the dead and the gods should be served. The master said, 'You are not able even to serve man.

How can you serve the spirits?'
'May I ask about death?'
'You do not understand even life. How can you understand death?'[9]

Other material in K'ung's writings and the anecdotes told about him suggest that he had little interest in the areas of speculation or divination. But there are two statements which are credited to him which do appear to show a direct link between K'ung and the *I Ching*. In *The Analects*, VII, 16, he says that if he were given extra years of life he would spend fifty of them studying the *I Ching* so as not to make so many mistakes. Then, in XIII, 22, he quotes directly from Hexagram 32. Some scholars have argued that these texts are suspect and must be later additions. Yet there seems to be no good reason why someone should have added them. It would appear that K'ung did have both a familiarity with and a high regard for the *Chou I*, but whether he then went on to write so much about it is highly unlikely. More probably what we have in the 'Ten Wings' are commentaries of the period from the fifth to the third centuries BCE which were given status by using the name of K'ung. This was a common practice throughout the early history of China.

There is one strong indication that, although K'ung probably was intrigued by the *Chou I*, he nevertheless did not work on it to the extent later supposed. The *Chou I* (or, as it became known, the *I Ching*) did not achieve the status of a Classic (which is what the word *Ching* in *I Ching* means) until about three hundred years after K'ung's death. While it seems impressive that K'ung mentions the *I*, it is equally interesting to note that none of the other major writers – Lao Tzu, Mencius, Hsun Tzu and so on – who wrote during the period of the sixth to the third centuries makes any mention of the book or its messages. Indeed, the earliest lists of the Confucian Classics, the five books, do not mention the *I Ching*. Instead they mention the four other books of the current list (*Shu Ching, Shih Ching, Li Chi, Ch'un Ch'iu*) and a now lost book called the *Yo Ching* (*The Classic of Music*). It is only in the lists compiled after the great Burning of the Books under the Ch'in dynasty (221–207 BCE) that the *Chou I* is listed as one of the Five Classics and achieves the title of *I Ching*.

It is in the record of the Burning of the Books in 213 BCE that we have our first clear sight of the *I Ching* and of its importance. The tyrannical ruler Shih Huang-ti used the military power of his state of Ch'in to crush and then unify the various minor states of China. His cruelty and iron rule terrified the people and even to this day his name is evoked as an example of authoritarian evil. Part of his tyranny was a desire to control not only the present and the future but also the past. To this end his Prime Minister put forward the following proposal:

I humbly propose that all historical records but those of Ch'in be burned. If anyone who is not a court scholar dares to keep the ancient songs, historical records or writings of the hundred schools, these should be confiscated and burned by the provincial governor and army commander. Those who in conversation dare to quote the old songs and records should be publicly executed; those who use old precedents to oppose the new order should have their families wiped out; and officers who know of such cases but fail to report them should be punished in the same way.[10]

Thus although the great Classics – being historical records or books of ancient songs – went to the flames or were only preserved as fragments hidden in walls and hideaways, the *I Ching* – a book of divination and therefore not considered contentious – survived. It is unique amongst the Five Classics in not having been damaged in this terrible time.

It is after this period, when the Ch'in dynasty had crumbled as fast as it had risen, that the *Chou I* became the *I Ching* and ranked alongside the older established Classics. Why? Again we can only look at the social forces at work at the time and see if there are any clues there.

The time of the Ch'in dynasty and the early years of its successor, the Han, was a period of great cultural and psychological shock and readjustment. Essentially the Chinese world had been brutally smashed apart. The order of obedience and the tenets of loyalty had been brushed aside, and the cruel, capricious and, even more disturbing, unpredictable nature of humanity had been laid bare. All the previous norms and structures of society had collapsed, of no avail against the onslaught of the Ch'in. For the first time for centuries questions arose about the reason and purpose of life. The stage was wide open for new ways of dealing with life and with the future. It was into this spiritual and cultural vacuum that divination in its popular form came. The rise of the belief in auspicious days and other fortune-telling practices associated with the calendar dates from this time and was much decried by scholars, who saw it as being an undesirable infringement on 'ancient ways'.[11] It is around this time that the practice of physiognomy began to exert a powerful hold on all levels of Chinese society – again filling the vacuum left by the collapse of the older values.[12] It is therefore not surprising that such an ancient book of divination should rise to a new level of authority. It is from this period that we can talk about the *I Ching* being essentially the book which we have to this day.

That something momentous had occurred is very clearly indicated by what then happened to the *I Ching*. Up to the second to the third centuries BCE we know of the book's existence and some hints about its role. However, they are, as we have seen, merely hints. True, they are sufficient for us to know that at various stages from around the Shang dynasty (1523–1028 BCE) through to the Burning of the Books in 213 BCE, a system and/or a book called *Chou I* was in use and considered to be of value and of antiquity. But what we also know is that, with the exception (if we accept the texts as authentic) of K'ung Fu-tzu, no other writer of any note paid the slightest attention to the book up to the start of the Han dynasty. Yet not only during the Early and Late Han dynasties (207 BCE–220 CE) did some of the most important philosophers turn their hand to commenting upon the *I Ching*, but over twenty different books on the *I Ching* have survived from this period to our day. Obviously the fact that it was now considered a Classic meant that it had status and was read by those who might not have concerned themselves with it in former times. This is seen in the frequent references to the *I Ching* in the biographies of leading officials during the Han dynasty. The histories speak of the *I Ching* as though it was an essential part of a scholar's training – which indeed it seems to have become. The sheer diversity of the commentaries from this period show the degree of speculative thinking which the *I Ching* attracted. Entire systems of physics, metaphysics and straightforward magic were declared to have been found within the *I Ching*. A mystique arose which may have been there in former times, but which now grew to be almost a philosophy in itself. It began also to be coloured by association with other important spiritual books such as the *Tao Te Ching*. For instance, take this statement made by Kuan Lu, an important scholar official of the Three Kingdoms period (221–280 CE): '"The fact is those who are thoroughly versed in the Changes do not discuss the Changes."'[13] This parallels the opening words of the *Tao Te Ching* itself: 'The Way that can be described is not the real, everlasting Way. If it can be given a name, it is not the real eternal name.'

The *I Ching* became the standard for all the civilized arts, from warfare through to painting. For instance, in the fifth century CE the artist Wang Wei opened his essay on landscape painting by saying that painting 'is not to be practised and accomplished merely as a craft; it should be regarded as of the same order as the images of the Changes.' [14] Entire theories of history were constructed on the model of growth and decay found within the *I Ching*. Historians looked for cycles within the lives of the dynasties and, as we shall see later, this cyclical pattern gave the Chinese a philosophical acceptance of change at the highest levels which provided a very helpful model for future centuries.

An interesting picture of how people saw the *I Ching* and what they expected it to be able to answer is given in the *Nei P'ien* of Ko Hung, a fourth-century writer who combined what to modern minds seems a strange mixture of scientific thought with quixotic mysticism and alchemy. In reply to a question about why the Five Classics do not mention how to become a divine being (a practice which religious Taoism sought to develop), Ko makes the following statement, which not only illustrates the status accorded the *I Ching* but also the limitations which at least Ko Hung felt it had:

There is no limit to what is not contained in the Five Classics, and there are a great many things about which the Duke of Chou and Confucius say nothing. My object now is to expound roughly one ten thousandth of this other material to you, and I will not be stopped even though you may ridicule me. It would be difficult to set forth a complete description of the whole process, and I therefore wish only to have you listen to a rough account.

Heaven and earth are the biggest things in creation. *The Changes*, composed jointly by nine sages, is sufficient to embrace completely yin and yang (the physical universe), but nothing more. Today, when we ask those who study this classic about the size of the sky, the breadth of the four seas, the extent of the universe in miles, where up and down end, who is doing the pushing or pulling when things revolve, the speeds of the sun and moon, on what the nine paths of the moon are mounted, the durations of darkness and light, the successive positions of the constellation Hydra, the swellings and shrinkings of the five planets, the 'hats and pendants' to the sun of partial and total eclipses of the sun and moon, the trespassings upon the 28 celestial mansions, the source of comets, the anomaly of vapour dartings, the omen in lucky stars and in Canopus, the failure of the north star to move, the solitude of Saturn in the east, the heat when the sun emits rays but chill when the moon reflects inward, the Milky Way's sparkling appearance when we look up at it, the waves and tides moving back and forth in varying magnitudes, the foreboding of joy or anger by the Five Notes and the Six Regulators in the Ten Trunks of the sexagenary cycle, the good and bad times indicated by the movements of clouds and the risings of vapours; certain comets, shooting stars, meteors, dartings, reddenings, comets over any of the four revered mountains, thundering meteors, and strange celestial phenomena sometimes proclaiming success and at other times failure – when we ask the specialists in *The Changes* about these things they cannot answer us. And when after that we turn to the specialists in *The Annals* (all four parts), *The Poems, The Writings of Old,* and *The Three Rites,* we again receive no answer. They say that there is no mention of these things in the standard classics.[15]

It is obvious that some people felt the *I Ching* ought to be able to answer all those questions. And it was against this sort of wild speculative use of the *I Ching* that later Confucian writers sought to defend the book's integrity. In particular, during the Sung dynasties (960–1279 CE) much of the more speculative material was banned as being unnecessary and confusing. Instead the Sung philosophers developed their own metaphysical speculations, but this time they sought to bring more traditional (as they saw it) Confucian ethical values to the book. Indeed, the edition of the *I Ching* produced by the Sung philosopher Chu Hsi (1130–1200 CE) became accepted as the standard orthodox edition and was not superseded until the Imperial edition of 1715. Yet while the philosophers worked to clear away the old editions which they felt obscured the *I Ching*'s true meaning, the alchemists of the same period were busy trying to use it as a handbook of chemistry in order to find the elixir of life. For instance, Ch'en Hsien-wei, a thirteenth-century writer, saw in the hexagrams *K'an* (29) and *Li* (30) a basic chemical formula.[16] One of the Five Classics of the scholar the *I Ching* may have been, but it was also seen as a legitimate area for theories arising from less orthodox disciplines. In a sense there has never ceased to be a battle between the at times quite stiflingly rigid interpretation by orthodox Confucians and the more open-ended use by Taoists and Buddhists. By the time of the Ming dynasty (1368–1644 CE) the *I Ching* and its commentaries of a Taoist nature had found their way into the official Taoist canon. This vast corpus of material, covering over a thousand volumes, contained a special section on the *I Ching* in the same category as the main magical and alchemical texts.[17]

There is a fascinating book to be written about what the various groups made of the *I Ching*, but this is not the place. It is perhaps sufficient for us to know how influential the *I*

Ching had become, and how anyone who wished to put forward a theory had to find some justification for it within the *I Ching*. What is pertinent to our interests is what happened in 1715. From the late Sung (*c.* thirteenth century CE) until 1715 the edition of the *I Ching* prepared by Chu Hsi was the standard one. In 1715 a new edition came out which superseded the Sung one and upon which all translations of the *I Ching* into European languages have been based. But why should a new edition be brought out then, and what interest did an invading foreign power have in this ancient Classic?

2
The West and the *I Ching*

西方人对易经看法

In 1644 the old Chinese dynasty of the Ming collapsed before the onslaught of a foreign power – the Mongolian hordes of the Manchu. Over the next decade the Manchu established their rule over the whole of China, and the Manchu dynasty, taking the title of Ch'ing, which means 'pure' or 'bright', settled down to rule. The Manchu were not Chinese: they originated from Manchuria and were different in looks, language, beliefs and customs from the Chinese. This was emphasized by the Ch'ing dynasty in various ways. First, all Chinese men were made to wear the queue as a sign that they were under the authority of the Manchu. As intermarriage and domestication of the Manchu took place, such marks of difference became increasingly important. After all, the Manchu only constituted 2 per cent of the population and yet they were the rulers. How could such a small group gain control and keep it without recourse to vast standing armies or policies of terror? This was the main problem which confronted the first two Ch'ing emperors, Shun-chih (Emperor from 1644 to 1662) and the great K'ang-hsi (1662–1723).

One main way of dominating China was to make the ancient texts speak for the new regime. Very early on in the reign of the Ch'ing opposition to and support for the Manchu focused on the Classics, and in particular on the *I Ching* with its cryptic messages about friends and foes, fortune and evil, and – in various hexagrams details of directions from which friends or enemies would come. Essentially the Manchu sought to show that they had the right to rule by drawing upon the traditional interpretation of the *I Ching* as given by Chu Hsi. As Immanuel C. Y. Hsu puts it in his book *The Rise of Modern China*:[1]

The emperor [K'ang-hsi] was particularly fond of the great Sung Neo-Confucian scholar Chu Hsi whose commentaries on the Classics he regarded as 'the grand synthesis of hundreds and thousands of years of untransmitted learning, capable of opening the minds of fools and children and of establishing the ultimate goal (truth) for a myriad generations.' ... To be sure, K'ang-hsi's sponsoring of Neo-Confucianism was not without political motive, for Chu Hsi's ideas of Grand Unification and the importance of honouring the ruler made his own domination of the state a matter of course. Opportunistic scholars in the country therefore flocked to the Sung Learning, i.e. Neo-Confucian School, while anti-Manchu scholars, favouring Han Learning, maintained an opposition.[2]

We know from K'ang-hsi's own writings that he justified many of his actions as ruler by recourse to the standards and values which he and his advisers read into the *I Ching*.[3]

One quite extraordinary effect of this pro-Manchu/anti-Manchu division amongst the scholars was the fact that those in opposition started taking the ancient classical texts apart and applying what we would call historical exegesis to them. They showed how certain long-accepted texts were in fact not as old as they were claimed to be. They shattered certain assumptions, which seemed to have been expounded from the earliest times, by showing that they were much later in date and had been added to older texts to justify the newer attitudes. This historical criticism was possible because in their own time they had to watch as the Classics were taken over by 'barbarians' – namely the Manchu – and used to bolster up their claim to authority over the Chinese themselves. It is within this context of political manipulation of ancient texts that we need to see the particular significance, which has never been properly understood in the West, of the Imperial edition of the *I Ching* of 1715.

The Imperial edition of 1715

So ferocious and so revolutionary was the historical criticism of scholars such as Yen Jo-chu, who showed the reputedly ancient text *Documents of the Shang Dynasty* to be a forgery, or Hu Wei, who claimed that the trigrams and hexagrams of the *I Ching* were Taoist inventions and had nothing to do with the original book, that K'ang-hsi, who prided himself on his classical learning, felt something had to be done to reassert the authority of the orthodox interpretations, in particular, the interpretation which bolstered up the right of his house to rule. Thus it was that the Imperial editions of the Classics were launched, including, of course, that of the *I Ching*. What we are saying, to put it quite simply, is that the edition which has been used by all Western translators, and whose commentaries have been viewed almost as though they were gospel, was in fact an exercise in political manipulation, foreign imperialism, oppression and vindication. The *I Ching* of

1715 is first and foremost a sociopolitical book published to support a particular line. Thus while it does indeed draw upon many of the great commentaries, the reasons for choosing some and not others or for emphasizing certain teachings and not others lie in the political game which was being fought – a game the prize for which was the right to rule. Therefore we should be very careful in seeing in the Imperial edition of 1715 an objective, totally unbiased document, apparently distilling for us, without prejudice, all the greatest wisdom of the ages about the *I Ching*.

Rather, we should view the *I Ching* as we would view any great writing: undoubtedly capable of revealing other dimensions of reality to us, but also shaped and developed by the particular society and needs of that society which gave it its current form. There is no disrespect in this attitude. Most Christians are able to view the Bible as both the Word of God and yet also to see that it has been variously interpreted by different people at diverse times for sundry reasons. Exactly the same approach can and should be applied to the *I Ching*, otherwise we find ourselves running the risk of absolutizing statements and styles which arose for reasons which no longer really need affect us.

Having said this, it is worth pointing out that most of the material used in the 1715 edition is of the highest quality and value and is, of course, capable of being interpreted in a variety of ways. But it is important to keep our critical wits about us!

To this day the Imperial edition of 1715 exerts tremendous influence. But while the ancient text of the judgements of King Wen and the lines of Tan remains unchanged, as does most of the material in the 'Ten Wings', the wider background commentaries to this edition give cause for concern. For the very tradition of state Confucianism and classical education which gave rise to these commentaries has now been swept away and almost entirely lost. The Empire has gone. The great academies have ceased to function. The assumptions underlying the commentaries are no longer relevant. Yet the *I Ching* goes on from strength to strength in the Chinese communities around the world, and now also again in China itself. This is why for our edition we have provided a new commentary which draws on this post-Imperial, post-state-Confucian world and on the way the Chinese themselves use the *I Ching* today.

In this survey of the stages through which the *I Ching* has passed it now only remains to look briefly at how the West has responded to the book and to ask a few pertinent questions regarding the sources of the teaching and style which have been the hallmark of the great translators of the text.

> Fohi, Founder of the Monarchy, composed before that time *Poems of this Nature,* but they were so obscure, that what care soever they took to put a good Construction on them, yet have they been fain to confess, that they were not intelligible.

So wrote Louis Le Comte SJ, a Jesuit missionary who lived in China during the last part of the seventeenth century.[4]

> This obscurity so unfathomable to the most learned Heads, hath given occasion to many Superstitions. The Bonze's [Buddhist priests] wrest them to a wrong use and make them say what they please; they are to them an inexhaustible Fountain of Fables and Chimera's, which they make use of, to cause the People to pin their Faith upon their Sleeve. However they have compiled a tome of them – the *U-kim* – which holds the third Rank amongst Classick Authors.

Obviously Le Comte could not fathom the *I Ching* and saw it merely as a collection of random sayings of such obscurity as to provide ample space for all manner of false speculation. And to some extent, as we have seen, he was right. But he failed to penetrate the heart of the *I Ching* – a difficulty which bedevilled all early attempts by Westerners to understand the book. While the moral and ethical teachings of figures such as Confucius were early translated into European languages by the admiring Jesuits, the *I Ching* had to wait until 1834 before it appeared in Latin under the direction of the Jesuits Jules Mohl and Paul Regis. This was a worthy but lumbering translation which did not claim to understand the book. The second translation, by a Rev. Canon McClatchie, was a disaster – primarily because he tried to use a crude methodology of comparative religion to make sense of it and in doing so utterly lost sight of its role, significance and history. It is best to draw a discreet veil over this edition. It is really with the famous translation by James Legge that the *I Ching* begins to make some mark on the West and, very importantly, the West begins to make a mark on the *I Ching.*[5]

James Legge and Richard Wilhelm

James Legge was probably the single most remarkable missionary to China of his age. Born in 1815, he arrived in

China in the early 1840s. By the 1850s he was already becoming known as a translator and interpreter of the Chinese scene and language. All the major translations of the Five Classics and the Four Books, along with countless other important Chinese works, we owe to Legge. But what was a Christian missionary (he later went on to be the first Professor of Chinese at Oxford) doing translating 'heathen' books? The answer quite simply is that Legge was no narrow-minded missionary. He saw in all the great creations of Chinese civilization the hand of God at work. His was an inclusive theology long before such thinking became acceptable. While most missionaries believed they were taking God to the Chinese, Legge believed he was bearing witness to a fuller experience of God, but that the Chinese had always had witness to and belief in God within their society and scriptures. His was a truly universal understanding of God which for him made sense of the good and wonderful things he found in Chinese literature and life. Thus when he approached the Classics, especially the *I Ching*, he did so in a sense of eager anticipation that he might find therein glimpses of God which had been vouchsafed to the Chinese in antiquity. Legge in his long introduction to the *I Ching* in *The Sacred Books of the East* (1882) tells how his first attempt to translate the book was not a success. He seems to have failed to find the key. However, by 1882 he had undertaken a new translation and the key is spelt out in his introduction. Legge had found God at work in the text and felt that he was dealing with, albeit in a rather confused way, a divine revelation not unlike that given to the Israelites – and at points about as clear! In this light he did his translation and it is for this reason that certain Chinese terms were translated or interpreted in a quasi-Christian way.

Before anyone, with the supposed benefit of hindsight, starts getting self-righteous about this, let us remember what an uphill task Legge had to face. As Le Comte's quote shows, the *I Ching* was dismissed by virtually all Western scholars of China as so much mumbo-jumbo. Indeed, when Legge proposed to the board editing *The Sacred Books of the East* that the *I Ching* should be included, he initially met opposition from some of its members who could see nothing of spiritual value in the book. It is precisely because Legge and after him the German translator Richard Wilhelm were able to make the *I Ching* sound vaguely familiar in a biblical way that the book came to be accepted by Western readers. This was a great service, but unfortunately later translators did not break free from this spoonfed approach to the book. In our edition we have sought to move away from the heavy language of the earlier translations, which has now done its job of getting the West to take the book seriously. Instead we have returned to a more faithful Chinese sense of the book. Consequently we have sloughed off much of the overweighty, metaphysical, biblical and overtly religious language which Legge and Wilhelm, heirs respectively to the wonderful but ponderous styles of the Authorized Version and Luther's German Bible, felt was essential.

It is Wilhelm's translation which above all others has influenced the Western attitude to the *I Ching*.[6] Wilhelm was a pastor to the German colonies in China. He arrived in the last years of the nineteenth century, imbued with the same approach to Chinese literature and beliefs that Legge had espoused: namely, that God was already present in China and that Christians should look to find him there, not seek to introduce him.[7] By the time Wilhelm came to do his translation it was quite acceptable to believe that, just as the Israelites had been given a special revelation of the name and true nature of God in the books of the Old Testament, so the Chinese at the same time had been given a similar revelation, but that this had been lost under the later layers of Buddhist and Taoist religion.[8] In particular it was believed that divine revelation could most clearly still be seen in the ancient Classics. Precisely because of the difficulties in interpretation, the *I Ching* was seen as the foremost ground for finding such revelation. It is important to stress that this was not seen as being exactly of the same kind as that given in the Old Testament. Rather, it was regarded as being distinctly Chinese in mode and style – but worthy of equally serious attention and reverence as the Old Testament revelation. It is out of this intellectual milieu that Wilhelm came. It is also perhaps important to note that other scholars had been looking at Buddhist texts in much the same way and had found exactly the same 'evidence' in those. For instance, the medical missionary Timothy Richard wrote a book called *The New Testament of Higher Buddhism* in which he sought to treat the great Chinese Buddhist texts as further revelations of the God who bore witness to the Israelites and came to earth as Christ.[9] Thus we should not be too surprised to find that the most famous translation of the *I Ching* reads with about as much ease as the Authorized Bible's version of the Book of Leviticus or the Letters of St Paul. In the mind of Wilhelm, subconsciously if not consciously, that is what any great religious or spiritual text should sound like.

There is one further point to make. Wilhelm in his introduction talks of his indebtedness to his teacher Lao Nai-hsuan. He says: 'After the Chinese revolution, when Tsingtao became the residence of a number of the most eminent scholars of the old school, I met among them my honoured teacher Lao Nai-hsuan.'[10] As we have seen, the 1715 edition was a conservative document drawn up to validate by ancient precedents, or supposed ancient precedents, the rule of the Manchu. Add to this the outlook of Lao and you have a very conservative view of the *I Ching*. Let us not forget that Lao was a displaced person. His world had collapsed, and vast, threatening changes were sweeping in. The old scholars either went with the new tide or were left high and dry. That this led to an increasingly conservative approach to the values and material of the old order is not in doubt. Anyone who has read books such as the autobiography of the last Emperor[11] or accounts of the fading glories of the Court between the revolution of 1911 and the late 1920s will agree that a sense of morbidity and fossilization comes powerfully across. The scholars of the old order were lost and sought refuge in ultra-orthodoxy.[12] It is in this light that we should understand the teaching which Wilhelm received from Lao and the context within which Wilhelm undertook his monumental translation and explanation. What Wilhelm presents us with is an at times moribund, arcane and antique explanation of the *I Ching* and its use. This has resulted in a rather difficult and complex translation and has created an unneccesary air of additional mystery around the book and how to use it.

Since Wilhelm there have been a number of attempts to provide a simpler edition. Two notable editions stand out, that of Alfred Douglas, *The Oracle of Change*,[13] and John Blofeld's *I Ching*.[14] Virtually all other translations are reworkings of Wilhelm by people who know no Chinese and little else apparently, and some are such individualistic interpretations of the *I Ching*'s 'ideas' as not to be worthy of the name 'translation'. Rather, they should be called something like 'vague wonderings on something loosely to do with an English translation we've read of a Chinese book called the *I Ching*'.

In this book we have gone to Taiwan, Hong Kong and other places of the Chinese Diaspora to find what contempory diviners and interpreters of the *I Ching* make of it. We have also examined scores of modern and contemporary commentaries on the *I Ching* – the ones held in greatest esteem by the current Chinese users of the book. From over forty of these we have selected four main ones which we have found to be in widest use and which capture best the continuing tradition and evolution of the *I Ching*. Our modern commentary is distilled from all these sources. After all, the *I Ching* is a Chinese book, so it seems only natural to ask the Chinese of today, the direct heirs of the tradition, what it means to them and how they use it. In doing so we are not out to prove any great theory about its worth, origin or place in religious literature. Of the team who worked on it, some believe in its word utterly, some find much in it is true, others think of it as an interesting ancient book. So let us now turn to how, if you were to follow the method used around the world by the ordinary Chinese, you should approach and use the *I Ching*.

3
Using the *I Ching*

易經的應用

In 'The Great Treatise', one of the 'Ten Wings' of the *I Ching*, reputedly written by Confucius, there is a description of how to consult the *I Ching*. This is by use of yarrow stalks, thought in themselves to have magical powers.

[The stalks] are manipulated by threes and fives to determine [one] change; they are laid on opposite sides, and placed one up, one down, to make sure of their numbers; and the [three necessary] changes are gone through with in this way, till they form the figures pertaining to heaven or earth.[1]

The use of yarrow sticks for divination purposes goes way back into Chinese history. The *Shu Ching* (*The Book of Historical Documents*) mentions them as being used in the Hsia dynasty (*c.* 2000–1523 BCE) and even earlier. In later times, after the death of Confucius, the most auspicious yarrow sticks were cut from those growing on the mound of Confucius's grave.

Certain translations of the *I Ching* include very full descriptions of how to use the yarrow sticks. Notable amonst these are those of Blofeld and Douglas.[2] As the old fifty-stick method has largely fallen out of use among the Chinese themselves, we do not intend to give more than a basic explanation of how it works. It is complex, difficult, and seen by most Chinese as an interesting antiquarian method. Wilhelm, learning from the old, displaced scholars, has given it prominence and the fact that the *I Ching*'s own commentaries carry a description of this method has lent it perhaps a greater significance than it deserves today. In fact, if one wishes to see what has become of the old method of divination by yarrow sticks, go to any temple and watch the believers using them. Usually 100 in number, these sticks are placed in a special metal or wooden container. After offering incense and other gifts to the gods, the believer kneels down and reverently asks the god to whom he or she is praying to give an answer to a specific question. Meanwhile the believer also shakes the container until just one stick falls out. This will be numbered. The believer will then go to a professional fortune-teller, who will give him or her a copy of the particular divination message indicated by the stick and traditionally associated with the god to whom the believer has been praying. The fortune-teller then interprets the message and the believer has received the god's guidance. Two examples of the kind of messages are given earlier (p. 15–16).

In the ancient *I Ching* system fifty sticks were used. By a complex process of dividing and subdividing them into groups, a number was finally obtained which indicated either a broken line – known as a yin line – or an unbroken line – a yang line. (The terms 'yin' and 'yang' are discussed more fully below.)

yin   yang

Starting with the bottom line of the hexagram, the sorting process was carried out six times in all, until all six lines had been obtained. Then, by looking up that hexagram in the book, the interpretation could be found.

In current Chinese use the system has been simplified to twelve sticks. These are marked, six with a yang line and six with a yin line. They are held in the hand and, after prayer and calming of the mind, six are drawn from the twelve. The first stick pulled out gives the bottom line, the second the next and so on until all six lines have been given. Thus is the hexagram revealed. As there is no way of distinguishing a particular line (see below), the whole hexagram is read. This system is not considered to be as good as the *Pa Ch'ien* system which we give on p. 41–5.

A second system is also commonly given in translations and this is the three-coin system. Before the revolution of 1911 Chinese coins were made as symbols of Heaven and earth. The round shape was Heaven, while the square hole in the centre was earth. One side had an inscription and this was seen as representing yin. Wilhelm describes the procedure for its use well.

Three coins are taken up and thrown down together, and each throw gives a line. The inscribed side counts as yin, with the value of 2, and the reverse side counts as yang with the value of 3. From this the character of the line is derived. If all three coins are yang, the line is 9; if all three are yin, it is a 6. Two yin and one yang yield a 7 and two yang and one yin yield an 8.[3]

By this system, as with the yarrow-stalk system, the person seeking advice derives a hexagram which he or she then looks up in the book. If the hexagram consists only of lines created by throwing either a 7 or an 8, then you simply

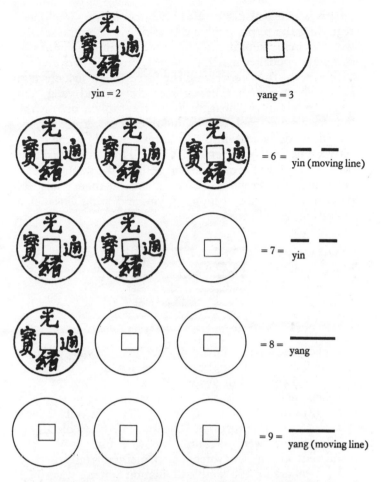

look up the hexagram given. If, however, you throw a 6 or a 9, then these are called moving lines and you need to look up not only the meaning of the hexagram but also the meaning of the particular lines which have these numbers. These are called moving lines because they can be exchanged for their opposites. By changing the lines from yang to yin or vice versa, a whole new hexagram is derived which is used to amplify the interpretation. (See Appendix 2)

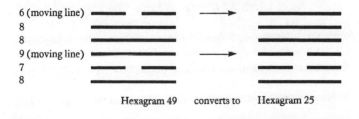

It is worth pausing here to give just a little more detail regarding the terms 'yin' and 'yang'. The Chinese see the world as being kept in motion by the dynamic unity of two complete opposites which constantly struggle to overcome each other – thus generating the force which sustains and moves the universe. These forces are yin and yang. Yin (represented in the hexagrams by the broken line) is the female, passive, cool, watery, moon element. Yang (represented in the hexagram by an unbroken line) is the male, active, hot, fiery, sun element. You will find in our text that occasionally a line is described as being in the wrong place – i.e. a yin line in a yang place. This is because there is an ideal pattern for the disposition of yin and yang lines in a hexagram, as follows:

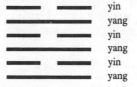

However, the adverse effect of a yin line in a yang place or vice versa is only of significance if the rest of the hexagram is itself a dangerous or awkward one.

When we came to work on this text, those of us who had been introduced to the *I Ching* by Western translations were in for a big surprise. The two methods discussed briefly above were certainly known, but both were dismissed. The ancient yarrow-stick method is only used by fortune-tellers for the temple divination systems described above. Any suggestion that this system might be regularly used today with the *I Ching* was met with surprise. It was rather like suggesting to a modern-day printer using web offset to print copies of the Bible that he really ought to be using a quill pen and doing it by hand. Historically accurate it might be, but it is not in current use. It was seen as being far too lengthy and convoluted. As we have said, the simplified version is used but not given too much credit.

As for the three-coin system – a look of pity came over various faces when we mentioned this. Such a cumbersome and awkward method! Why should we bother ourselves with such a long-drawn-out system when there was the *Pa Ch'ien* – or eight-coin – system? This system appears to be the one most commonly in use at present and introduces a whole new way of using and listening to the *I Ching*.

But before we explain this system it is important to

mention one other use of the *I Ching* which has also been missed out of previous translations and explanations. In the main the Chinese use the *I Ching* for quiet meditation and reflection. If a copy (usually wrapped in yellow) is kept in the home, it is only asked direct questions at times of great difficulty or moments of great change. It is not resorted to regularly, but is regarded as the most important oracle, to be consulted only in times of crisis. Chinese homes have a copy of the *T'ung Shu*, the Chinese almanac, which contains numerous divination systems which can be used for more mundane matters.[4] The *I Ching* is used most often as a book of general wisdom, studied quietly in the evening, perhaps in order, as one person put it to us, 'to understand the way of this world a little better'. It is still treated with the respect which it is accorded when a question is to be put to it. Namely, you wash your hands before touching it, offer incense and generally prepare yourself so that you are in a calm, receptive and reflective state of mind. And then you read the *I Ching* in much the same way as a Christian might undertake personal study of the Bible or a Muslim the Koran.

However, if you do wish to put a question to the *I Ching* it is most likely that you would go to a professional *I Ching* reader. He will help you interpret the meaning of the hexagram and of the particular line you have been given, for under the *Pa Ch'ien* system you are directed not just to a specific hexagram, but also to a specific line. There are no moving lines, only one line – the line of change – from which you will receive your message.

Naturally we do not expect our Western readers to resort to a professional Chinese *I Ching* reader. This is why we have called this translation *The Fortune-Teller's I Ching*. We hope that, with its clear translation of the ancient Chinese texts and with its modern commentary, this book will be your own portable fortune-teller. For Chinese readers, we hope that it will assist you even if you also go to a professional diviner.

The *Pa Ch'ien* Method

The chart on p. 42 shows the eight trigrams set out in a circle in the order given by Fu Hsi. Note that the Chinese, when setting out the cardinal points, always place south at the top.

For the *Pa Ch'ien* system you need eight coins of the same denomination. One of them should be marked in some way – by an inkspot for example or with a wax crayon

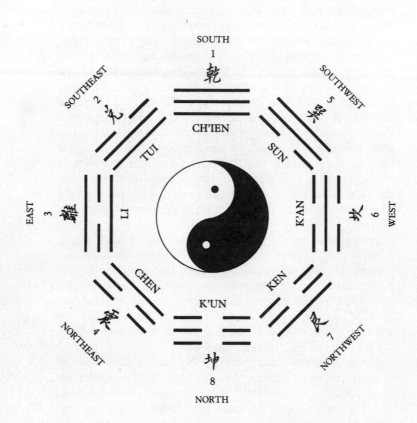

- to differentiate it from the others. It is customary to keep the coins used for divination in a special container alongside the bound copy of the *I Ching*. The inquirer should be in a suitable frame of mind, ready for what the *I Ching* might have to say. He or she should then phrase the question in a suitable way: for example, *Is it good for me to continue in this*

line of business with my present colleagues? Then he should take the eight coins and turn them in his hands until they are mixed up. Then, taking a coin from his hand, he places it on the *Ch'ien* trigram, the south one, no. 1. Then he takes a second coin and places it on the *Tui* trigram, southeast, no. 2. Then on to *Li*, east, no. 3; then *Chen*, northeast, no. 4. If the marked coin has not come up yet he goes on to *Sun*, southwest, no. 5; *K'an*, west, no. 6; *Ken*, northwest, no. 7; and finally, if necessary, *K'un*, north, no 8. *If at any point the marked coin is placed upon a trigram, he stops, because that is the trigram which forms the bottom three lines of the hexagram which will provide the answer to his question.* So let us imagine that he has placed the marked coin on *Tui* – southeast, no. 2. That means that the first three lines of his hexagram are First Nine, Second Nine and Third Six. (In the three-coin system 'Nine' indicates a moving yang line and 'Six' a moving yin line. In the *Pa Ch'ien* system there are no moving lines and 'Nine' simply means a yang line and 'Six' a yin line.)

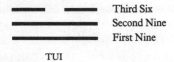

TUI

He now shuffles the coins again and again lays them out one at a time around the circle of trigrams. Let us say that this time he finds that the marked coin lands on *Li* – east, no. 3. This means that the top of his hexagram is formed by the *Li* trigram, giving him Fourth Nine, Fifth Six, Top Nine.

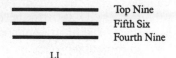

LI

Tui and *Li* combined form the hexagram *K'uei*, Hexagram 38. (See Appendix 2)

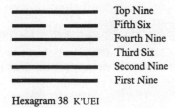

Hexagram 38 K'UEI

Having ascertained the hexagram it now remains to find the *line of change* which will give the answer to the inquirer's question. To find the line of change, remove two unmarked coins from the eight. Then, mixing up the six coins as before, place them in an ascending line, thus:

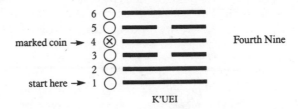

It is important to start at the bottom and work up. When the marked coin appears, that is the line to refer to. So let us imagine that the marked coin comes up fourth – thus giving line four in the *K'uei* hexagram, Hexagram 38.

The inquirer then turns to Hexagram 38 in the book and reads the judgement of King Wen: 'Opposition. There will be good fortune in minor matters.' He then looks at the text for Fourth Nine, the line which the coins have indicated is the one for him. In this instance the ancient commentary by Tan, Duke of Chou, tells him: 'Alone in opposition. He can be confident when he meets the top man. There is danger but there will be no mistakes.'

It is then customary for the inquirer to ask a fortune-teller or diviner to explain the meaning of the hexagram and the line. The fortune-teller would first turn to his favourite commentaries and ask a few pertinent questions. Then he would give a clear and fairly thorough explanation. In previous editions of the *I Ching* the diviner's function was in part fulfilled by the traditional background commentaries which often drew on historical or mythological events and people. Our new commentary which replaces them attempts to be more personal in style, using the direct form of address, such as you would receive if you visited a fortune-teller. In the example we are considering our commentary to Fourth Nine advises you: 'At the moment you may feel isolated from others. Give yourself time to understand people. With the help of a wise man you will develop a long-lasting friendship.'

To sum up, to find the answer, first read the judgement of King Wen and the associated commentary for the hexagram; then read the lines of Tan and the associated commentary for the line of change. And that is it! No moving lines, no complex system. Just a very simple method which the diviners feel opens up the inquirer to the rhythms of the universe. We shall look at this and other philosophical and religious ideas behind the *I Ching* in the next chapter.

Having outlined the method of using the *I Ching* it is necessary to make some comments about our own translation and the nature of the material itself. We have not included the 'Ten Wings'. This is of historical interest only and of little relevance to the way the *I Ching* is used today, except as background reading or by the more advanced reader for meditation. The traditional commentaries, which have been replaced by our new commentary, are not used by modern diviners, who have, in any case, incorporated this sort of information into their own commentaries. The judgements of King Wen, and the lines of Tan, the Duke of Chou, are set in italic in our text, to distinguish them from the commentary.

There is much in the language of the *I Ching* which comes directly from a Chinese setting in a way that makes it difficult for non-Chinese to understand. For instance, the colour yellow always stands for the Emperor, as this colour was reserved for him or for things to do with Heaven. The term 'Heaven' itself is not to be taken to mean the dwelling place of some divine being such as God. It is a more abstract term and is defined in the next chapter. Tortoise shells, meaning divinational skills, should now be intelligible to the reader. The *I Ching* is, of course, sexist and reflects the patriarchal values of those who composed it and those who used it. We have not tampered with this patriarchal language, as to do so would be to lose the book's original flavour, and to disguise the fact that it is still used today to bolster up what many would now see as sexist attitudes.

Finally, the lines of the hexagrams have traditionally had various virtues and attributes ascribed to them. It is particularly important in the context of this translation to understand the following relationships within the hexagrams. The first line is associated with the fourth, the second with the fifth and the third with the top. In each trigram the middle line is the line of authority or responsibility, holding the trigram together. When the trigrams are combined, the middle lines have specific titles and roles which are frequently mentioned in many of the commentaries. The second line is seen as being a low official, perhaps the mayor of a town. The fifth line is seen as being the Emperor, ruler of all of the people. Between these comes the fourth line, which is described as the Prime Minister. This is responsible for maintaining the flow of authority from the Emperor to the mayor. Weakness in any of these positions is not good, as you will find in the commentary.

Having described how the *I Ching* came into being and how it is now used, it is time to turn our attention to its meaning and the significance of asking it a question. It is not enough to know how to ask; you must know what sort of answer it will give and how that answer should be understood. Anyone who is looking to the *I Ching* to tell them what the future will be or to give them an immutable prediction of their fate had best seek another book, for the *I Ching* will not do that. So let us explore what it will do.

4

The Philosophy of the
I Ching

易經的哲學

There is an enormous gulf between Chinese and Western thinking about fate. In the West it has been traditional to interpret fate as being a fixed, unalterable fact. If you are fated to kill your father and marry your mother, as in the Oedipus story, then no manner of schemes or strategies would prevent you fulfilling your fate. Fate is something fixed from on high. For instance, in Greek thought it was fixed by the gods, who played games with people. Later, despite the insistence in Catholic Christianity on the role of free will, doctrines of fate or, as it was called by the followers of Calvin, predestination came to exert a powerful pull back to the fixed and unbending concept that life was planned for you, not by you. Modern research into religious and moral attitudes in the West today shows how popular this kind of fatalism is, removing as it does the need to be ultimately responsible for your own actions and your life. Unfortunately many Westerners have now begun projecting this theory onto the divination systems of the East, not least of which has been the *I Ching*. This has happened despite the insights offered to Western readers by people such as Carl Jung in his introduction to Wilhelm's edition. A similar problem is also to be found in attitudes to other Chinese systems such as physiognomy.[1]

The Chinese concept of fate is very different. It is captured in the word *ming*. This has the sense that, while certain things in life are fixed, such as the cycle of birth, growth, decline and death, other aspects are not, and it is the responsibility of each individual to decide how he or she should live. Now this might sound rather vague and unstructured. But again we need to understand the Chinese context of such an idea. In Chinese thought the entire system of life is determined by the two forces, yin and yang. These are opposites which, through their opposition (light/dark, male/female, hot/cold, etc.), create a union of extremes – a creative tension. In doing so they give rise to inevitable forces which roll through the cycles of events. And these events are not static. They are the rise and fall of forces. By positing opposing forces, a dynamic tension, which is totally absent in Western ideas of fate, is created of which the most appropriate description is 'change', *but change within an overall pattern*. Thus, the great Chinese historical romantic novel, *The Story of the Three Kingdoms,* opens by saying: 'Empires wax and wane; states cleave asunder and coalesce . . .' and ends: 'All down the ages rings the note of change, for fate so rules it, none escape its sway.'[2]

Within this idea of change there is the concept that each individual can either flow with the sway of change and thus personally benefit, or go against the flow and be crushed. This is not really seen as making 'moral' decisions, because the very force which creates these changes is impersonal; it is usually described in the *I Ching* as 'Heaven'. While there is considerable discussion as to whether this term originally referred to a personal deity,[3] in the post-Confucius text of the *I Ching* it refers to the ultimate force behind the world and all life. The role of Heaven and also of man is clearly seen in this quote from the commentary on the *Ch'un Ch'iu* (*Records or Annals of Spring and Autumn*) – one of the Five Classics. This commentary, called the *Tso Chuan,* was written somewhere between the fourth and the second centuries BCE. In describing the role of *li*, which has the connotation of correct and righteous behaviour, the writer, Tso, gives a very clear picture of how, by behaving according to *li,* man can be in harmony with and thus be both harnessed by and harness for himself the changing state of nature.

'Allow me to ask,' said Chien Tzu, 'what we are to understand by ceremonies [*li*].' The reply was, 'I have heard our late great officer Tzu Ch'an say, "Ceremonies are founded in the regular procedure of Heaven, the right phenomena of earth, and the actions of men." Heaven and earth have their regular ways, and men take these for their pattern, imitating the brilliant bodies of Heaven and according with the natural diversities of the earth. Heaven and Earth produce the six atmospheric conditions, and make use of the five material elements. Those conditions and elements become the five tastes, are manifested in the five colours, and are displayed in the five notes. When these are in excess, they ensure obscurity and confusion, and the people lose their proper nature. The rules of ceremony were therefore framed to support that nature.'[4]

There is another very important idea within the *I Ching,* or rather behind the *I Ching*. This is spelt out in the following quote from the *Shih Shou Hsin Yu* (*New Discourse*

on the Talk of the Times), which dates from the fifth century
CE.[5]

> Mr Yin, a native of Chinchow, once asked a [Taoist] monk,
> Chang Yeh-Yuan, 'What is really the fundamental idea of the
> *Book of Changes* [*I Ching*]?' The latter answered, 'The
> fundamental idea of the *I Ching* can be expressed in one single
> word, Resonance.' Mr Yin then said, 'We are told that when the
> Copper Mountain collapsed in the west, the bell Ling Chung
> responded, by resonance, in the east. Would this be according to
> the principles of the *I Ching*?'
> Chang Yeh-Yuan laughed and gave no answer to this question.

The idea that there is an essential sound or resonance
within the universe is not unique to the Chinese. The
Hindu concept of the sacred sound 'Aum' being the essence
of the universe lies behind the style and purpose of Hindu
chants and literature. And it is this idea of basically putting
yourself in touch with the essence of the universe through
the use of chance that lies behind the *I Ching*. If there is an
essential pattern and flow to the universe, and if it is
possible to tap into this at any time, then it simply remains
to find the correct or best method of doing so. By allowing
random chance to rule in the use of coins or sticks, you are
able to open yourself to the flow of the universe and to be
guided not by some divine figure, but by the inevitable
forces of which the *Tso Chuan* speaks, while putting
yourself in resonance with the fundamental idea expressed
in the *Shih Shou Hsin Yu*.

Having done this, by the apparently random selection of
sticks or positioning of coins, you are now in touch with, or
resonating with, reality. But you are also part of the triad of
Heaven, earth and man which actually creates this reality.
You are not a puppet on a string, but one of the puppeteers.
Here is, again, the great divide between Chinese and
Western notions of fate. An interesting story concerning
another system of divination, physiognomy, will illustrate
what we mean.

There once was an old monk who was very learned in the
ways of physiognomy, and he had a young servant by the
name of Sung Chiao. One day the old monk looked closely
at the face of Sung Chiao and saw that he had only a month
to live. Being a compassionate man, he dismissed the boy
and sent him home to his family, telling him to spend at
least a month on holiday. As the boy journeyed, knowing
nothing of his supposed fate, he saw a group of ants floating
helplessly downstream on a piece of wood. Using bamboo
poles and straw, he built a bridge to the piece of wood and

helped the ants to crawl ashore, thinking nothing of it other than that it had been an act called forth from his kind nature. He continued on his way. When the month was over he returned to his master's house. His master was amazed to see him still alive and asked him what had happened to him in the last few weeks. The boy told the story of his going home and how he had saved the ants. Then it was that the old monk realized that nothing was irreversibly fixed by Heaven, and that acts of compassion and of goodness could change anyone's future.

What the *I Ching* tells you is how, following the pattern you have established for yourself, you will fare if you continue along this line. It also gives suggestions as to what steps may enable you to realign yourself with the deeper pattern which you may well be running against. But always the advice is one which 'forth tells' rather than foretells. That is, *it tells you about yourself*, and this forthright comment gives you a fairly clear idea of *how you will go if you continue along the path you are now on*. But it does not really foretell, that is, tell you what is going to happen. This emphasis on 'forth telling' is very important. To misunderstand this is to misunderstand the entire *I Ching*. In the modern commentaries in this translation this is made very clear.

So enjoy and respect this book. It is one of the oldest books of China, and one of the oldest of its divination systems. As such, it needs to be seen and used within the terms by which it is traditionally understood. In giving you the ancient text, so full of meaning after many thousands of years of use, and the contemporary commentaries, expressions for today of the ancient traditions of interpretation, we hope that the true nature of the *I Ching* will be made accessible.

THE HEXAGRAMS

CH'IEN

The Origin

HEXAGRAM 1

The origin. Continuing through. Harmonious. Correct.

The Way of Heaven is the basis for human life and it is the way in which we begin our life, since it is the beginning of everything. The six lines of this hexagram control the world, and everything develops correctly as a result. Harmony is created and the whole world is well and at peace.

A wise man usually follows the *Ch'ien* hexagram so he can live in an honest and courteous way. *Ch'ien* makes everything flourish; it makes everything grow well and it helps everything live properly. *Ch'ien* combines Heaven in its upper and lower trigrams. It is therefore pure yang. The yang spirit ensures that everything goes smoothly and properly.

The dragon is the symbol of both yang and the wise person. He therefore has the power to control everything. If he appears on the bottom line he is hiding in very deep water; in the middle line he is in a field, and at the top he is flying through the sky. Therefore he is constantly changing. If the yang spirit is not in harmony or is trying to compromise, the wind roars and torrents of heavy rain fall. If the yang spirit seeks harmony, then the wind is light, the rain is gentle, and all is peaceful.

Line of Change

FIRST NINE

Do not use the diving dragon.

This line represents the eleventh and twelfth months, when yin is at its height and yang is barely visible. Be like the spring sunshine which waits until the worst of the winter weather has passed away. Do not do anything important today because you are not in control.

SECOND NINE

The dragon is seen in the field. It is helpful to see the great man.

Although you are well educated and honest you do not want or cannot achieve power. You must be trustworthy in everything you do and say and all will be well.

THIRD NINE

This wise man is active all day long, but in the evening he is watchful. There will be great difficulty.

This line is correctly placed. You are hard-working and your actions have won the respect of others. Moreover you are vigilant and can distinguish right from wrong. You can stay where you are without any anxiety.

FOURTH NINE

He is bouncing up and down in stormy waters. The sage says that he sometimes leaps up and sometimes down. There is nothing wrong in this as long as evil is avoided.

This yang line is in a yin position. You are restless because you are in the wrong position. You will show maturity if you change the direction of your life without losing your friends.

FIFTH NINE

The dragon is flying in the heavens. It is good to see the great man.

Be like an emperor who is kind and considerate to those under his command. In return the respect of those who work for you will deepen.

TOP NINE

A group of headless dragons appears. There will be good fortune.

Because the yang line is in a yin position there will be disaster and sadness.

K'UN

Success

HEXAGRAM 2

Great success. A wise man is virtuous and proper, like a strong but gentle mare. When he is faced with a task he can only succeed if he takes things slowly and carefully, not trying to be first. If he is happy to follow others, all will be well. It is important to have friends in the south and west, but they can be lost or forgotten if they are in the north and east. A wise man must remember to draw strength from proper conduct, and by doing this he will be fortunate.

Ch'ien, the first hexagram, is pure yang, and *K'un*, the second, is pure yin: since yin and yang interchange with each other, all things are born from the union of *Ch'ien* and *K'un*, Heaven and earth. So the first two hexagrams relate and interact with each other. *K'un* represents the earth nature and it is situated under *Ch'ien*. The six lines of *K'un* are even, while the six lines of *Ch'ien* are odd, therefore *Chi'en* and *K'un* conceive everything that exists. The things which are produced in Heaven are conceived on earth and things which are born from earth end up in Heaven. *K'un* is gentle and soft, and the symbol of a female horse is used to signify its calm and peaceful nature. *K'un* represents everything which is born, develops and changes, and during these stages there will always be good results. The power of *K'un* is suitable for healthy growth and vitality of life. At the same time it is gentle and looks to *Ch'ien* as its controlling power.

Line of Change

FIRST SIX

He is walking on newly formed frost. Freezing conditions are on the way.

2 K'UN

Confucius used this comparison of frost and ice to illustrate how everything is subject to change. When cold weather is on the way you stock up with firewood so that you can keep warm; in the same way you must plan and prepare for difficulties ahead so that when they arrive you are able to cope.

SECOND SIX

Square, straight and strong. Everything will work out well without any effort.

Your worth and virtue are shown through the standard of your work. You have a good and wise heart, but you must demonstrate this to others through your actions. *Ch'ien* and *K'un* work harmoniously and you too must keep an inner and outward balance.

THIRD SIX

He does not reveal his virtue for all to see, but nurtures it within himself. He has the opportunity of serving the Emperor and will perform his tasks with great success.

Before making any move, think carefully. If you are in a reasonable job and promotion passes you by, it is not because of your lack of skill or intelligence. Work diligently and peacefully at your job. Eventually things will work out well.

FOURTH SIX

A sack has been sealed up so that nothing can flow in or out. There will be no blame and no praise. What is done is done.

K'un is gentle and quiet; it holds and protects rather than moves. Like *K'un*, which is inherently powerful and does not need to display its strength, you will not come to harm if you handle things around you carefully.

FIFTH SIX

Imperial yellow undergarments. There will be excellent fortune.

Like a man who wears an Imperial yellow garment, which is a sign of nobility and fortune, you have a generous, warm and accommodating nature. Deal with everyone politely and kindly and you will keep your high position.

There are dragons involved in a ferocious fight in the desert. The blood that flows from their wounds is Imperial yellow.

The sky is cloudy, the natural colour of the universe has changed. Blood is scattered on the earth. Because yin is at its strongest point, distressing times are on the way. Your relationships are unstable and you are driven to breaking point. You must follow the correct path.

CHUN

Birth Pangs

HEXAGRAM 3

Birth pangs. He will be successful if he behaves properly. Beware of starting a new venture without giving it sufficient thought. It will be useful to enlist the help of an experienced person.

The *Chun* hexagram is made up of the trigrams for thunder and water, *K'an* and *Chen*. These also stand for male and female, for Heaven and earth, yin and yang, and so on. Although it is possible for these opposites to live together, they could easily erupt into arguments and unhappiness. Thus *Chun* is seen as meaning a potentially dangerous and confused time. Like birth, everything is just beginning. It is just like a new child who has great potential for a happy and successful life. But there will be many dangers and difficulties lying ahead and the child has to summon up strength and courage to overcome these challenges. Like seeds which lie in the soil, the opportunity for growth is there, but only by being firm and resolute will the seed rise out of the difficult soil and grow to full height. Keep going despite all the difficulties and you will eventually succeed.

Line of Change

FIRST NINE

The way ahead is blocked. Remain firm. Act sensibly. Listen to the advice of someone more experienced.

You have very little responsibility because this line is the lowest position. You have a strong, fine spirit and attract people who will give you good advice. You appreciate people's difficulties. You will succeed with their support.

The horses are outside the village but are not allowed inside. The people think they are robbers. They have come to collect the bride. The bride remains firm and rejects the union. Ten years later she marries and has children.

The woman refuses the offer of marriage because her suitor is of a lower class than she is and her parents do not approve. Likewise you must not rush into a mismatch, be it marriage or work. If your staff are not happy, then the organization will not be successful. It is far better to wait for the right moment even if this means working hard for a long time before you can enjoy the fruits of your success.

THIRD SIX

The hunter, stalking a deer, is drawn into the forest. He failed to ask the forester for help and is now lost. The wise man can see the dangers which lie ahead. He knows it would be foolish to continue so decides to give up the chase.

Although you have a weak character, you are in an important position, and therefore will easily fall into danger. If you are greedy and thoughtless you will end up in deep trouble. Be like a wise man who listens to others' advice.

FOURTH SIX

The woman has lost control of her carriage and the horses are running away with her. The man who wants to marry her is nearby and she calls for his help. To advance will bring good fortune. All will turn out well.

If you are determined to succeed there will be initial difficulties. Be patient and accept a certain amount of compromise; eventually you will be lucky. Try to assess everything properly and give others time to learn that you are trustworthy. Follow this advice and you will be successful.

FIFTH NINE

He is finding it difficult to grant the favours people expect of him. Wise behaviour brings success when dealing with minor affairs. Any attempt to deal with major issues will bring misfortune.

If you help others quietly and without fuss you will be

respected, but if you show off you will be resented. Proud and selfish attitudes will only backfire on you.

TOP SIX

The man is in complete disarray since his chariot horses have gone into full retreat. He cannot hold back his tears and begins to weep.

Just as everything seems to be running smoothly there is suddenly chaos and confusion. Plan ahead with an eye to pitfalls. Do not give up, despair or run away from difficulties, but patiently carry on until you succeed.

MENG

Rebellious Youth

Rebellious youth. I do not look for the rebellious and ignorant child; it is he who looks for me. When he asks me for an oracle I will answer him. But when he asks me a second and third time he becomes a nuisance. I refuse to answer his requests. It is helpful to be consistent and well behaved.

Meng is a combination of *Ken* and *K'an*, the mountain resting on water. Although the upper and lower trigrams are in their correct positions, the lines inside *Meng* are in a confused and chaotic state, thus rendering them obscure. *Meng* can be compared to a young child who has not yet understood the complexities of the world; but a time will soon arrive when these difficulties will be eased and the picture becomes much clearer. A strong mind and will are needed to carry a person through these confusing times, and the wise man stresses the importance of education and effort when trying to break through. People cannot be forced to study. A wise man should gradually nourish his student's mind so that information is slowly accumulated and understood. The water which flows underneath the mountain has to cross many rocky places before it meets other streams and eventually becomes a river. In the same way a growing child faces many trials which are overcome step by step through having a strong mind and an honest nature.

Line of Change

FIRST SIX

It is good to use punishment in order to banish ignorance. This helps free the mind from its bondage. Too much punishment brings about humiliation.

蒙

You can only learn through experience and not through force, like someone who commits a crime because his mind is confused and then finds himself in prison. The prison officer who releases the prisoner is also responsible for freeing the prisoner's mind from the confusion which led him into crime. Everybody has their own distinct way of learning. Success is possible once you understand the actions and thoughts of yourself and others.

SECOND NINE

Be patient with the ignorant, since this will bring good fortune. It is good to listen to the requests of women. A son is able to run his family.

You will have a happy home if you establish a stable relationship with your children. Give them a good education, be there when they need you, and your family life will prosper.

THIRD SIX

Do not become involved with a woman who will easily give herself to a man with money. Such behaviour will bring misfortune.

Do not let yourself be seduced by greed and desire. You will be left feeling sad, embarrassed and full of remorse. The holy man advises you to think ahead.

FOURTH SIX

It is sordid to be constrained by ignorance. It will bring regret.

You face many problems for which you must take responsibility. You are sad, alone and full of remorse. Do not waste so much time on idle pastimes but spend time preparing for the future.

FIFTH SIX

The innocent child. There will be good fortune.

You may not be clever, but you are warmhearted and honest. Seek the advice of a good teacher who will encourage you. His guidance will help you be successful.

Punishing the ignorant child will do no good. It is better to protect him.

When you are confused and do not know which way to turn, take advantage of the educational opportunities on offer. You will be peaceful and happy when you find the right path.

HSÜ

Patience

Patience. Confidence and sincerity will bring prosperity. Virtue will encourage good fortune. There is much to be gained by crossing the great river.

The *Hsü* hexagram is a combination of *K'an* and *Ch'ien*, water and Heaven. Heaven produces all things and water feeds all things. Without them everything would die. The sunshine emanating from Heaven is yang and the rain is yin. In as much as the earth needs light and water, we too need help from those around us. We have to have food, clothing, housing and transport, we need family support, intellectual stimulation and personal honesty. The *Hsü* hexagram tells us that these things take time, but with confidence and patience we will eventually receive what we need.

Crossing a mountain or a river is difficult but not impossible. The journey will be successful if you go slowly and with care. *Hsü* represents our necessities for life, and since *Ch'ien* comes before *K'an*, we must have the strength of mind to cross uneven and dangerous areas or else our way will be blocked. *Ch'ien* is awkward, but as soon as these dangers are passed we reach the bright Heaven of *K'an*. The *Hsü* hexagram is in the shape of a cloud rising to the sky. Although the cloud drifts above us, it rises from the earth. The cloud and the earth are interdependent. In much the same way our physical and emotional needs are dependent upon each other. There has to be a balance between serious thought and enjoyable activities.

Line of Change

FIRST NINE

He is waiting out in the open country. A lot can be gained by

Heaven ceaselessly provides the earth with everything it
needs and you must work in harmony with Heaven. Heaven
provides our food, light, housing and transport, but this all
takes time. Heaven is always successful, so do not try to
alter the path which has been set for you. You are heading in
the right direction but do not be greedy or impatient.

SECOND NINE

*He is waiting on the sand. He will have to tolerate gossip, but in
the end he will be very fortunate.*

You should help those who are in a lower position than
yourself when they need help. Be like sand which can be
used to form embankments or dykes across wet areas. Sand
is more fragmentary than stone but harder than soil and can
be used to alter the texture of stone or soil. You too must act
as a link between people of higher and lower positions. Like
sand you must be strong and accommodating even though
others may abuse or blame you.

THIRD NINE

He is waiting out in the mud. This allows the enemy to arrive.

The world around you is like wet ground. When soil
becomes wet, it easily turns to mud. However, it is better to
cross mud than try to cross the water. These are violent,
hasty and awkward times. Now is the time to be cautious
and considerate. Swimming across a river may be quick,
but it is better to dirty your feet than to drown. Do not be
arrogant; it will only cause trouble.

FOURTH SIX

He is waiting in a place of blood. He must escape from the pit.

You have to sacrifice your own ambitions in order to help
others. This yin line lies between two yang lines. The three
lines together are shaped like a grave. New life will come
from the sacrifices you are willing to make. This is also the
time to use your own judgement and if necessary stay at
home and avoid direct actions. It will be best to come out
when everything has settled down.

FIFTH NINE

*He is waiting amongst the food and drink. Good fortune will
come through virtue.*

5 HSÜ

We all need to eat and drink to keep alive. However, extravagance can bring an end to success. Be in control of yourself and your desires. Live frugally and all will be well.

TOP SIX

He goes into the pit. Three guests arrive who have not been invited. Treat them well and in the end there will be good fortune.

This is a time of great danger. The line talks of falling into a pit. You are in great difficulties. People as yet unknown to you will come to your assistance. If you are wise and courteous, even to strangers, things will go well for you.

SUNG

Contention

HEXAGRAM 6

Contention. He is confident in the face of opposition.
Respectful behaviour will bring good fortune. If he persists to
the bitter end there will be misfortune. It is very helpful to see
the great man. It is not a good idea to cross the great river.

The *Sung* hexagram contains *K'an* and *Ch'ien*, water and
Heaven. The *Sung* hexagram means contention, and it
shows how you have to struggle to succeed. *Sung* does not
compromise but fights to the bitter end. Take care not to
lose the honour or respect of others. If the argument or
lawsuit is successful then everything will have worked out
well. But should the argument or lawsuit fail then you must
wake up to the fact that you may be at fault. If you feel that
you have been unjustly accused then seek the advice of a
wise man to help you prove your innocence. Do not,
however, try to become involved with too many legal
wranglings since this will only result in misfortune. Your
opponent will be a very cunning person. The upper trigram
Ch'ien means strength and the lower trigram *K'an* means
violence or cunning.

The top part of the *Sung* hexagram belongs to the power
which ascends to Heaven, and the lower part to water which
runs down into the ground. The top part of the hexagram
can be likened to a great judge, while the lower part is like a
great gulf which is full of dangers and pitfalls. Do not try to
cross over the gulf since there are two natures running in
different directions. Confucius used this example to show
how you should consider everything carefully before
making any major decisions.

Line of Change

FIRST SIX

*He never pursues the issue. He has to tolerate gossip.
Eventually he will be lucky.*

The first six remains at the bottom of the *Sung* hexagram
and indicates argument. It should be easy to control the
situation since it is only a small matter brought on by a
slight misunderstanding. Deal with this minor problem
with care and patience and all will run as smoothly as
before.

SECOND NINE

*He does not have the strength to face the challenge. If he decides
to run back home to the three hundred families of his city he will
bring no harm upon himself.*

This line stays in the main position of the lower part of the
hexagram. Because you are stubborn, you will find life
difficult. Because you are impatient, the issue will end up in
court. When you realize that you have made a mistake you
will run back home in order to escape embarrassment. As a
result the lawsuit will be dismissed. One day's patience can
avoid a hundred days of worry.

THIRD SIX

*He stays in the correct place. There are great difficulties at the
moment but everything will work out well in the end. If he
should happen to be in the king's service he will not achieve all
that he hoped for.*

The top line of the lower hexagram is in a yielding position.
By acting honourably you will be fortunate. Someone who
maintains the family honour and obeys his superiors will
have many good opportunities.

FOURTH NINE

*He does not have the strength to face up to the challenge. He
retreats and studies the way fate deals with people. He changes
his attitude and finds peace in virtuous behaviour. There will
be good fortune.*

A small upset may occur but it is better to control your
anger and cultivate a calm and respectful nature. By doing
this you can continue along a peaceful path.

By attending in the law court extremely good fortune will follow.

This line is in the correct position in the *Sung* hexagram. It is like a wise judge who listens carefully and then passes fair sentence. You should put an end to quarrels so that friendships can develop.

TOP NINE

The leather belt of status may be given to him but it will be taken away from him three times in one morning.

The winner of the lawsuit deserved this judgement. He is given a hero's belt as a reward. But it is much wiser not to encourage people to bring quarrels to court since this results in endless legal wrangles. It is important to clear up any legal arguments as soon as possible.

SHIH

The Army

The army. Everything is correct. Nothing will go wrong if the leader is wise and experienced.

This hexagram is a sign of powerful people, particularly in the military field. They not only take responsibility for protecting individuals but also for protecting the country. Since troops usually appear in large regimented groups they seem stern and majestic, but individually they are kind and caring. A commander has to be chosen and it is important to elect a man who inspires respect amongst soldiers and citizens alike. The commander must work for the benefit of others and not for his own gains, and at all times must maintain honour and integrity. Whoever has responsibility for guiding people, whether they be a commander or a teacher, must always be stern but honest.

The *Shih* hexagram combines earth and water in the trigrams *K'un* and *K'an*. The earth bears all things while water nourishes all things. Thus the people and the animals are cared for and healthy. This can be compared to a crowd of people who, when massed together, have great force. But numbers are useless unless there is a leader who is able to earn their respect and fire them with enthusiasm.

The *Shih* hexagram represents a group of people, but the fact that one yang line is operating with five yin lines is an indication that a leader will arise from the people. There is a possibility that this leader will not always be obeyed by his followers; although they may look obedient on the surface there could be hints of jealousy underneath. However, these troublesome elements are in a minority and the leader maintains the respect of those whom he guides; all will work out well.

Line of Change

FIRST SIX

The army marches off after receiving its orders. It will be disastrous if these orders are wrong or not well thought out.

Think carefully before making important decisions. An army is well organized and disciplined so that the normal life of the citizens is not disturbed. Unless you maintain discipline and order you will have chaos and unhappiness.

SECOND NINE

There is good fortune since the commander is at the centre of the army. He did not make any mistakes. The king honours him three times.

This is the commander's or official's line and the best position for a leader. However, do not get ideas above your station. Remember there are greater leaders above you to whom you are responsible. Remember this and act accordingly.

THIRD SIX

The army has incompetent leaders. There will be misfortune.

This line has three meanings. The first is that of a commander who has lost authority and therefore his army loses the war. The second refers to many leaders who all issue commands at the same time; thus their followers are in total confusion. The third meaning speaks of many dead soldiers. Unless things are properly ordered there will be chaos. Do not rely on the confusing decisions of many people. Do not be rash or reckless in your actions.

FOURTH SIX

The army retreats. There are no mistakes.

Do not start anything new. Stay where you are and be careful. This does not mean that you will fail but that things take longer than usual to return to normal.

FIFTH SIX

There are many different species of birds in the field. Now is the time to sieze them to avoid mistakes. The eldest son is the leader of the army. Although a younger son acts wisely he will certainly fail in the role of commander because evil will befall him.

You should be like a ruler who never gives orders directly to his army but always through an aide. When you choose such an aide, choose someone close to you – just as the ruler chooses his eldest son. However, even the most able person cannot control idle officers. It is risky to employ people with little experience. Always think carefully before appointing someone for an important task.

TOP SIX

The great prince is in complete charge. He chooses men to be rulers of countries, and others he appoints as the heads of powerful families. He does not give any of these appointments to weaker men.

This is the Emperor's position. From here he rules his empire. Always be like an emperor. Choose people whom you know to be capable. Leave the more run-of-the-mill jobs to those less capable.

PI

Unity

HEXAGRAM 8

Unity. There will be good fortune. When he asks the oracle about his fortune he is reassured. Those who are concerned will gather together at the right time. Those who arrive late will be unlucky.

This hexagram which combines *K'an* and *K'un* – water and earth – has only one yang line, in the middle of the top trigram. The yin lines are like a crowd which supports and honours an emperor. It is not unusual to find people who break the law since they have not been given a good education. These people will eventually be a source of trouble. The *Pi* hexagram signifies a large crowd of people who will be very successful if they all work together towards the same goal. The upper trigram is *K'an*, which is quiet and calm, but the lower trigram is *K'un*, which has a dangerous nature. *K'an* is suited to a quiet atmosphere, and should it move it will fall into danger. This can be compared to a crowd of people who are pushed together for too long. In the end some will become annoyed and quarrelsome. Although difficulties may be a nuisance at the beginning, they have to be ironed out quickly in order to avoid real problems. Cooperation at all levels is important in order to run a successful enterprise, and all problems must be approached in the correct way. Just as water and earth combine together in the hexagram so men must work together in harmony.

Line of Change

FIRST SIX

Confident actions result in unity. Confidence is like an overflowing cup which will eventually bring a variety of good fortune.

Trust and sincerity are important in this line. Be true and

75

honest and you will be fortunate. Kindness and warmth are essential for the success of your relationships.

SECOND SIX

Unity develops from the inner self. Good fortune will result from righteous behaviour.

Any friendship or partnership which you have with two or more people must be based upon pure and honest intentions. When your feelings come straight from the heart your friendship will be a good one.

THIRD SIX

He looks to unscrupulous people for unity.

Do not succumb to superficial flattery. If you do not choose your friends with care you will suffer.

FOURTH SIX

Unity is sought with those outside his close circle. Wise behaviour will bring good fotune.

Make a point of assisting someone in a higher position – just like a prime minister who obeys his emperor's will.

FIFTH NINE

The need for unity is becoming obvious. The king hunts the wildfowl on three sides only; he leaves the fourth side open for their escape. The local people were not instructed properly. There will be good fortune.

You must be like a wise man who goes hunting both for pleasure and sport. When he hunts he blocks in the animals on three sides but always leaves the fourth side open so that they may escape. Those who want to escape can do so, while the others are killed. Do not force things on other people. Use the best aspects of your personality to form friendships with those who wish to be with you. Draw them to you voluntarily – do not hedge them in.

TOP SIX

There is nobody to lead the united group. It is an evil time.

A small group of people should be able to organize itself without too much difficulty. If you are in a large group look to someone you respect for guidance. Always organize yourselves efficiently at the beginning. Mistrust and anger are easily aroused but adequate preparation will avoid them.

HSIAO CH'U

Holding Back the Less Able

HEXAGRAM 9

Holding back the less able. Progress and prosperity will develop. Clouds approach from our lands to the west but they do not bring rain.

Hsiao Ch'u's lower trigram, *Ch'ien*, is strong and obstinate, and is unable to have any bearing on the first yin line of the upper trigram *S'un*. This is why it is hard for virtue to develop at first. However, you can be successful if you are strong and tough on the inside but open and yielding on the outside. Someone who combines these two elements will be fortunate both in friendship and in business.

Although there are heavy black clouds coming in from the west, there is, as yet, no sign of rain. However, prepare for a heavy downpour. As yet the dark clouds have not received enough power from Heaven to produce rain. Likewise not enough preparation has been made on earth. Small savings may have been made but they are not enough to benefit everyone.

The combination of *S'un* and *Ch'ien*, wind and Heaven, produces clouds moving across the sky. Just as a typhoon cannot maintain its force for long, a loud and boisterous man cannot always hold sway. A wise man is like a gentle breeze which causes the clouds to drift slowly and the sun to shine. Thus he keeps all things well balanced through his intelligence and his forgiving nature.

Line of Change

FIRST NINE

He returns to the true path. Why should he be blamed for this? There will be good fortune.

9 HSIAO CH'U

You have been led by bad company. Turn your back on these people and return to old friends and familiar ways. This will bring you good luck.

SECOND NINE

He is lured back. There will be good fortune.

Now that you have returned to the path, take the role of leader. Use your experience to help others grow in honesty and strength. By changing your ways, good fortune will follow.

THIRD NINE

The spokes in the carriage wheel are broken. The husband and wife turn away from each other.

If the spokes of a wheel are jammed or the wheel brake is lost the carriage will be out of control. Likewise a quarrel with your spouse causes bad feelings. Do not be over-obstinate. You are like a husband and wife who refuse to agree on anything.

FOURTH SIX

Have confidence. The risk of bloodshed passes and fears disappear. There will be no mistakes.

You must be like this one yin line which is at risk from attack by all the yang lines. Remain calm and peaceful. Carry out your duties. The Prime Minister turns to his Emperor for advice and you too must work closely with someone in a position of authority. Be sincere and alert. Carry out your work honourably and everything will turn out well.

FIFTH NINE

The feeling of confidence is like the security of being bound together. He has ample resources close at hand and can draw his neighbours to him.

Develop good contacts with those around you, like a rich and respected man who keeps in close touch with his family. If you are willing to help, you will be respected.

When the rain falls everything stops, but virtue continues to flourish. The woman who behaves wisely is still in danger. It is nearly full moon. The man who ventures forth at this time will cause or create evil.

Life will become a little more peaceful now. It is like the relief everyone feels when the rain comes out at last or your car is finally repaired. You are like a husband and wife who have ceased quarrelling and whose love returns as strongly as before. The holy man says, 'Do not be greedy if you are successful, otherwise you will cause evil!'

LI

Walking Carefully

HEXAGRAM 10

Walking carefully. Although the man treads on the tiger's tail he is not bitten. There is success.

The *Li* hexagram combines Heaven and the marsh, *Ch'ien* and *Tui*, which represent the father above and the younger daughter below. Legend says that *Li* is the foundation of virtue. A civilized society must be well organized. Rules should be judged according to *Li* and all people should be both virtuous and moral. This is the mark of a true man.

This hexagram uses the tiger to describe man's obstinate and cruel nature; those who follow such a man will easily be harmed.

Line of Change

FIRST NINE

He is walking along his normal path. As long as he continues to do so there will be no problems.

Whatever you do, be well mannered and well behaved. Be sincere and honest and you will not make any mistakes.

SECOND NINE

He walks on the path which is smooth and easy. The peaceful hermit will be lucky, if he acts honourably.

You must be like an official walking along a straight road. He carries out his tasks efficiently and honestly. You will always be successful if you are happy and honest.

THIRD SIX

The one-eyed man can see; the lame man can walk; but the man who treads on the tail of the tiger is bitten and will have bad luck. The army officer behaves in this way for the benefit of his great ruler.

The holy man says that a half blind and lame man can look but not understand, can walk but is not able to follow the right path. Do not try to go beyond your capacity. You will cause trouble if you think your authority is greater than it actually is.

FOURTH NINE

He walks on the tail of the tiger. He will eventually be lucky if he is careful and cautious.

You are working for a harsh master. At the same time you are surrounded by cunning colleagues just waiting to see you fail. Be careful and wise, and tread warily.

FIFTH NINE

He walks resolutely. Although his behaviour is correct he is surrounded by danger.

You are like this line, which is in an ideal position. You should be quick and decisive. Always be modest and honest because arrogance easily upsets others.

TOP NINE

Look at the path which is taken and examine the resulting good luck. When everything is fulfilled there will be great fortune.

Watch carefully what is happening, and if you discover mistakes or malpractice correct them immediately. Good fortune will be yours.

T'AI

Benevolence

Benevolence. The lesser has disappeared and the greater is yet to come. There will be success and good fortune.

This hexagram combines *Ch'ien* and *K'un,* Heaven and earth. Through their mingling together all things grow. *Ch'ien* is strong inside whereas *K'un* is positioned outside and is willing to accommodate. This particular combination will produce peace. *Ch'ien* and *K'un* can be likened to a man and a woman who live in harmony. As the man is strong and the woman yielding they can work for the same goal and can live together in true harmony. *T'ai* enables good to overcome evil. The wise man runs his business carefully and is considerate towards those under his command. Thus he becomes stronger and his business prospers. The foolish man can only fail since he cannot challenge the power of the wise man.

Line of Change

FIRST NINE

When grass is pulled up it brings other stalks with it. Persevere. There will be good fortune.

The sage advises people of like mind to join together. When you pull out one grass it brings others with it; in the same way your needs are linked with the needs of others.

SECOND NINE

He bears with that which is uncontrolled. He is confident and crosses the river without using a boat. He does not forget the things which are far away from him and does not worry about friends. In this way he will keep to the middle path.

You are now united with everyone regardless of race and distance. Cooperation, determination, patience and perseverance can overcome the greatest difficulties.

THIRD NINE

Peace cannot exist without disruption. He cannot go without coming back. The man who is steadfast will not be blamed. He is not sorry but confident. He enjoys his good fortune.

Although Heaven and earth are far apart they can unite in spirit. Your life is like a spinning wheel – fortunes may vary but life continues. If you are really to be trusted you can pass safely through these dark and evil times.

FOURTH SIX

There is disruption and bustle. He does not rely on his own finances but turns to his neighbours. He puts his confidence in them. He does not withdraw from them.

Although your life may be uncomfortable, do not live beyond your means. Extravagance and arrogance encourage others to act similarly. Be on equal terms with other people and treat them with respect. The sage warns against bad habits. He urges you to behave properly in order to help others.

FIFTH SIX

The Emperor Yi gives his younger sister in marriage. This blessing brings great fortune.

Men and women must work together with mutual respect. When a woman rules the country she chooses a man as Prime Minister. He offers advice and help in difficult times. Likewise you should know who you need to complement your skills.

TOP SIX

The city wall collapses into the moat. Do not summon the army. He tells the people of his own country what is happening. Nevertheless, proper behaviour still causes distress.

In peace time defences crumble. The city becomes vulnerable to attack. You must not be like the citizens who have become lazy and indifferent, thus putting their country at risk. Be prepared for problems. Do not become complacent.

P'I

Obstruction

Obstruction. Evil men block the path of progress. Events turn out badly for the wise man even when he acts correctly. The great are leaving and the less important ones are arriving.

This hexagram is the opposite of the *T'ai* hexagram. *Ch'ien*, Heaven, is on the top and *K'un*, earth, is on the bottom so that the upper and lower trigrams are drawing away from each other. They are drained of energy and their source of power is blocked. This is a dangerous and hopeless time. Peace has disappeared and disruption is on its way. The wise man maintains his dignity through these difficult times, but even he suffers. People may be accommodating in private, but outwardly they are stubborn, so there is a notable lack of cooperation. It is like scattered sand which cannot bind together. Events are taken over by selfish men, and wise men must lie low in case they are set upon. The wise man should have strong willpower and refuse to cooperate with those who do wrong. Even in times of hardship the honourable person should not be greedy or extravagant.

Line of Change

FIRST SIX

Newly pulled-up grass will bring up other stalks which are attached to it. Firm and correct actions will result in progress and good fortune.

Stop being selfish and withdraw from those around you. Although the country is governed by selfish and corrupt men do not let yourself be drawn into their world. Stand up for your principles. Follow a wise leader who will sweep these men away and turn evil into good.

He is guided by patience and endurance. The lesser man will be lucky and the obstacles which lie in the great man's path will lead to success.

Corrupt leaders can easily take over a country. If you want order to return you must be strong and willing to take control. Evil cannot stand up against truth and justice.

THIRD SIX

He bears with his shame.

Corrupt leaders have damaged the country's reputation and brought shame upon its people. They are to blame for the present situation. Do not burden yourself with guilt for this. It is beyond your control at the moment.

FOURTH NINE

He is wise to follow the demands which are made by destiny. When his companions come they rejoice in his blessings.

This line is like a bright, clear lamp which gives light and brings good fortune. You must be like a prime minister who obeys his emperor's commands and passes them on to those beneath him. A country can be reformed through cooperation.

FIFTH NINE

The obstruction is removed. The great man is fortunate. He should take care and be on his guard against destruction. He should act as though he is bound to a mulberry bush.

To be a good leader you must always rely on others. Everything will improve when you carry out your duties honestly and wisely.

TOP NINE

At first there were obstacles. They have now been cast aside and there is rejoicing.

Evil men are trying to seize power but they will soon be scattered. The time is ripe for a good leader to bring his people back to peace and prosperity. This takes time and effort. Do not expect immediate results.

T'UNG JEN

Companions

*Companions. Friends will be found in the remote countryside.
He will be successful. It is helpful to travel across the great
river. The wise man will reap rewards if he behaves correctly.*

This hexagram is a combination of the trigrams *Ch'ien* and
Li, Heaven and fire. It is a good mixture and refers to a
group of people who are of the same mind. Although this
hexagram represents fellowship, there will naturally be
differences amongst the group, so one wise, strong man is
needed to maintain the coherency and harmony within the
group. The five yang lines have a yielding nature which
matches well the obstinate nature of Second Six which is a
yin line. The lines work well together. They have the same
heart, mind and resolution. Their coherence enables both
the country and the citizens to prosper. The sage says that
the citizens have elected an excellent leader who can
distinguish right from wrong, so he and his followers will
act as though they were one body.

Line of Change

FIRST NINE

*Friendships should be developed with people at the door. There
will be no mistakes.*

Those behind the door of your own house will be well
known to you, whether they are friends, family or
neighbours. Make plans with the people you know and
trust. If others are willing to cooperate, open the doors of
your house and your heart and welcome them in. It is not
important whether they are rich or poor, it is their honesty
and virtue that count.

SECOND SIX

Friendships formed within the family bring humiliation.

You can only be strong when you all leave the home and work with others for a common cause. The sage cautions against divisions and arguments within such groups.

THIRD NINE

He hides the weapons in the grass on top of a hill. He does not attack for three years.

There are always people within a group who are secretly plotting. Stand away from the common run so that others can see you are truly to be trusted. Sort out internal arguments and you will all succeed.

FOURTH NINE

He scales the defences of the city but is unable to attack. There will be good fortune.

Be patient, not rash. Be like an army which does not attack for fear of hurting the citizens inside the city wall. The citizens eventually surrender. Others will respect your patience.

FIFTH NINE

At first his companions cry out, then they weep and finally they laugh. The great army conquers all in its path. They meet together.

An army may suffer setbacks but its spirit is not diminished. When peace is declared tears turn to laughter. Although your life may be full of difficulties remember your friends. Trust in other people helps overcome setbacks.

TOP NINE

Good friends are to be found in the countryside. There is nothing to regret.

A good leader will not want to renew the fighting because he knows how much suffering this brings to the people. He knows, however, that there are always cunning citizens ready to rebel if they are given the opportunity. Not all people can be of the same mind. Therefore form friendships with those who are like-minded.

TA YU

Many Possessions

HEXAGRAM 14

Many possessions. It bodes well for him to have numerous possessions and great success.

Ta Yu means that everything is ripe, just waiting for the harvest. The upper trigram, *Li*, is successful and the lower trigram, *Ch'ien*, has great productive power. These combined trigrams are a strong source of nourishment. Although *Ch'ien* is obstinate, *Li*'s brightness will shine through *Ch'ien*'s awkwardness. Fifth Six is a yin line which is in a powerful position, so the other lines look towards it for guidance. Second Nine is a yang line and has an obstinate nature. Fifth Six can be compared to an accommodating and caring woman and Second Nine to a strong and creative man. Together they will have a happy and successful family. In order to achieve success and prosperity man must live according to Heaven's way. He must destroy evil and encourage honesty.

Line of Change

FIRST NINE

He is wise not to approach dangerous areas or people. If he understands the way things work there will be no mistakes.

Despite difficulties, this is a good time. Develop close relationships, curb your arrogance, avoid evil. Cultivate that within you which you know is best.

SECOND NINE

The heavily loaded wagon will be safe whichever way it goes.

This line is like a heavily laden wagon which carries food to the poor villages. The Second Nine is strong and bountiful because Heaven is enriched by *Li*'s fire. It is an abundant time and you are strengthened with new energy.

THIRD NINE

The duke offers his labours to the son of Heaven. A lesser man could not do this.

Heaven produces everything which the earth needs, and you must share your wealth both with the ruler of the country and its people. Do not be like a mean man. He does not share his wealth or pay his debts. He is neither welcomed nor trusted by others.

FOURTH NINE

He does not use up his strength. There will be no mistakes.

Do not become preoccupied with riches or status. Avoid those who are greedy; trust those who are honest; spend your money wisely.

FIFTH SIX

His self-confidence sets an example for others. Such dignity will bring good fortune.

The second, fourth and fifth lines all agree with each other and work together. You will have good fortune if you follow their way.

TOP NINE

He is fortunate since Heaven is his personal protector. There is nothing wrong in this.

Heaven's unfailing goodness can be compared to the sun which rises each day with renewed warmth. Heaven produces a harvest once every year without fail. Follow Heaven's guidance and lead a life of truth and devotion.

CH'IEN

Modesty

Modesty. The wise man will eventually succeed in everything.

Ch'ien combines earth and mountain in the *K'un* and *Ken* trigrams. The obstinate yang line is crouched in the lower trigram and *K'un* is able to be accommodated in the upper trigram. *K'un* is not arrogant even though it is in a higher position, and the yang line is content in its lower position. *K'un* is used to describe a wise and respected man who is successful because of his courteous behaviour. This hexagram also has relevance for less important people who give to the poor and are never reliant upon those in power. Such people are known for their humility and politeness.

Line of Change

FIRST SIX

The wise man carries out his duties with true modesty. Because of his unassuming nature he is able to cross the great river. There will be good fortune.

By being both well mannered and modest you will succeed in business. Even though you are faced with daunting problems you will be successful.

SECOND SIX

Modesty speaks for itself. Good luck will come from proper conduct.

Everyone is inspired by your conduct and speaks highly of you. Your manner is polite, you are respected and your business is growing.

The superior man succeeds because he is a person of merit and honesty. Thus he has good fortune.

This is the only yang line in the hexagram. Be careful! However successful you are, you must always be modest or you will be overtaken by others.

FOURTH SIX

Modesty is an admirable quality.

Do not be overwhelmed by flattery. If you are in an important position behave like a prime minister. Pay attention to those above and below you and help those who need you.

FIFTH SIX

He is not considered rich by his neighbours' standards. The time is right for invasion. Everything he does will work to his advantage.

If you are in an important position you must not be afraid of responsibility. If necessary, fight to protect others and help them prosper. Gather round you those you trust and respect.

TOP SIX

Humility has made itself known. It is the right time to attack both city and the country.

A wise leader forms an efficient army to protect his people. You too must gather trusted people around you. If you have true understanding you will know how to deal with attacks and accusations.

YÜ

Enthusiasm

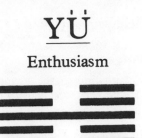

Enthusiasm. The time is right to appoint princes and give orders for the army to approach.

The *Yü* hexagram is progress and prosperity. It has a generous nature and makes a comfortable and pleasant world for others. The hexagram combines *Chen* and *K'un*, thunder and earth. The First Nine of *Chen* is a yang line and all the others are yin so they obey this line. The yin and yang cooperate with each other and there will be a successful period. *K'un* is likened to a mother and *Chen* is likened to an older son. The son does not initially wish to obey his mother but eventually they come to a mutal agreement. In order to cooperate and develop you must adjust yourself to the character and actions of others. It is important that a group of people develop harmony and enthusiasm so that together they may progress. It is like the harmony which is inherent in the cycle of nature or the movement of the stars.

Line of Change

FIRST SIX

He shows enthusiasm. There will be misfortune.

This line is weak and lacks support. Similarly you are not in a position to be boastful or extravagant. This attitude will only cause trouble.

SECOND SIX

He is as solid as a rock. He does not wait until the end of the day. His wise behaviour brings good luck.

Do not be fooled by those who live a life of extravagance and indulgence. Be as steady as a rock. Only then will you clearly see the pitfalls and recognize the right moment for action.

THIRD SIX

He raises his head with enthusiasm. This only brings regret. Delays will result in sorrow.

Be careful where you put your energies. You will be courting danger if you ignore the poor and fawn upon the rich.

FOURTH NINE

The source of enthusiasm is also the bringer of success. It is better for him to gather friends around him than to spend his time worrying.

Be like the ancient lord Sai Pak who lived during the Yin dynasty. Although he was wealthy and powerful he treated everyone equally. This is Heaven's way. By following it you will win respect and achieve success.

FIFTH SIX

Although he is very ill he perseveres and does not die.

Life is very tough for you so you have to conserve your energy and only act upon really important issues. Even an extravagant emperor can be restrained by a sensible prime minister.

TOP SIX

His enthusiasm is misguided. As long as he has the strength to change direction there will be no problems.

Too much time spent on pleasure will eventually ruin you. *Ch'ien*'s strength of character is now at work and your bad habits can, in time, be cured.

SUI

According or Agreeing With

Agreeing with. Great success. It is helpful to behave with propriety. There will be no mistakes.

The *Sui* hexagram combines the active nature of *Chen* with the quiet nature of *Tui*. *Chen*'s character is like that of an elder son and *Tui*'s is like that of a daughter, and so they correspond well. Both have an accommodating nature and *Tui* follows *Chen*'s guidance. All obstinacy and selfishness have been abandoned in favour of virtue. *Chen* is thunder and *Tui* is marsh. The surface of the marsh is as calm as a mirror, but when the thunder rolls the surface of the marsh ripples with the thunder's strength. Once thunder has filled the sky the rain begins to fall upon the marsh, which in its turn nourishes the surrounding land. The marsh is prepared to follow the thunder's action. The time is right for the thunder to roll, and right for change. Every day there are new developments and the old will be replaced by the new. The wealthy Emperor is likely to be extravagant, but his Prime Minister stops this. There are serious problems which restrict you, but acting in accordance with others brings good luck. Everything will run well as long as you behave properly.

Line of Change

FIRST NINE

The official changes. He is fortunate because of his wise behaviour. He is credited for going out through the gate to join his friends.

This line is in command of the *Chen* trigram, and like this line you must listen to the opinions and requests of those in

94

your charge and also abide by your own decisions. Do not listen only to like-minded people but listen to those who hold different opinions. This will help you to mature and grow.

SECOND SIX

He becomes attached to the young boy and rejects the older and wiser man.

You are shy and modest and may find yourself in the wrong company. Try not to lose contact with wise and helpful people.

THIRD SIX

He becomes attached to the older and wiser man and rejects the small boy. By following such a course he will find what he is looking for. He will benefit by following the righteous path.

Get rid of people who exert a bad influence on you. This may upset you at first but you will not regret it.

FOURTH NINE

Dogged perseverance is bad but agreeing with others brings fortune. His confidence in the path ahead is founded on true understanding. Can you find anything to blame him about in that?

You are in a position of power and therefore open to corruption. Your position is like that of the adviser to the Emperor. You have the opportunity to be successful but if you make the wrong decision you could easily fail. The decision lies in your hands. Do not be arrogant, obey orders. Be trustworthy and reasonable, listen to others and all will be well.

FIFTH NINE

He is confident in that which is good. There will be good fortune.

Because this line is in the Emperor's position you must do everything properly. Put your trust in someone who is honest, sincere and wise. Follow good advice and you will be very lucky.

17 SUI

He is bound down by strong links. The king brings fortune to the Western Mountain.

Your success has reached its limit and you have received every possible benefit. Now is the time to celebrate with your friends. Your success and fame will naturally continue.

KU

Decay

Decay. Crossing the great river will bring good fortune. Check everything carefully three days beforehand and three days afterwards

This hexagram has a rebellious nature. It combines *Ken,* the mountain, and *Sun,* the wind. The wind can blow in any direction, causing devastation of farmlands and houses, but it can also be gentle and harmless. After a time of disorder and decay order will return, but only after a period of careful deliberation. All the main aspects of society may have been destroyed and lives lost, in which case a strong moral leader is needed. He will be respected as a mountain is revered by the people. Using civilized means he will sweep away the devastation, destroying the opposing forces. From this all things may be able to start anew. Heaven's way is made up of endings and beginnings; both should be given time and care. Confucius says, 'Seven days come and go – that is Heaven's way, constantly renewing and recycling.'

Line of Change

FIRST SIX

The son sorts out the chaos which is caused by his father. As long as he is competent he can solve these problems without difficulties. Although there are immense problems everything will work out well in the end.

If you are making changes keep an eye open for all possible dangers. Be like a son who has helped his confused father out of difficulties. Be careful and alert, especially when you are changing things, and all will be well.

18 KU

SECOND NINE

The son has to sort out the chaos caused by his mother. He should not be overzealous in this.

A mother who is in trouble may not always accept her son's help. Likewise there are times when your help is spurned. Nevertheless set an example through your obedience in the hope that things may change.

THIRD NINE

The son sorts out the chaos which his father caused. There is very little to repent and he will make no mistakes.

Too much enthusiasm is better than none at all. Your minor problems will be smoothed out.

FOURTH SIX

He tolerates the chaos caused by his father. If he continues in this way he will be humiliated.

You should not hold back too long in offering advice, even if you find it embarrassing. If a son is too embarrassed to offer his father advice, the family business could collapse.

FIFTH SIX

The son is praised for sorting out the chaos which his father caused.

The situation may appear hopeless, like a father who is ruined financially and whose name is disgraced. Be like a son who works hard to retrieve his father's money and pride. Continued effort and determination will bring good results.

TOP NINE

He does not work for the king or his lord since he wants to serve a higher ideal.

A father cannot always depend on his son when faced with problems. He should now retire. You, too, cannot be expected to face difficulties and problems for ever. Even when you retire your experience can help others. A sage may withdraw from the world but even he sets an example for others.

LIN

To Draw Near

HEXAGRAM 19

To draw near. This is a time of great success which is helped by good behaviour. The eighth month is an unlucky time.

The *Lin* hexagram heralds a time of great encouragement and development. The yang spirits rise up from the earth and transform the spring wind which helps all things to grow. Lin combines *K'un* and *Tui*, earth and marsh. The marsh provides moisture for the earth, which in its turn gives life, but it can only do so when the rain falls. The wise man has received a good education; now it is his turn to encourage others with his wisdom and sincerity. In the same way as the marsh provides life-giving moisture, he gives endless consideration and guidance to others. In the *Lin* hexagram the obstinate Second Nine works well with the accommodating Fifth Six. Together they follow the way of Heaven.

Line of Change

FIRST NINE

He draws close to his friends. He will have good luck if he behaves wisely.

You must be like this line which moves forward in cooperation with Second Nine. Do not be carried away by popular trends. Since your actions influence others make sure that the person you work with is both honest and tough in his resolve.

SECOND NINE

It is to his advantage to draw close to his friends. Good luck will come.

You are stern and upright. You understand how transient life is. Not everyone will agree with the way you lead your life, but you will be lucky.

THIRD SIX

He will not suffer setbacks if he does draw close. He will not make any mistakes if he thinks his activities through properly.

Do not be complacent. You will lose your money and reputation if you are careless and overindulgent. It is not too late to change your ways.

FOURTH SIX

Nothing will go wrong when he arrives in great style.

The upper and lower trigrams, earth and marsh, are in harmony. You too should be able to work harmoniously with others. When you are open-minded you will find people who are not only able but also sincere.

FIFTH SIX

Like an eminent leader, he approaches wisely. He will have good fortune.

Choose people who are capable and responsible. In present-day China the ordinary people who are given positions of responsibility are respected by everyone. Because this line works well with anything which is right, you should be happy to give and take orders. Others will trust your decisions.

TOP SIX

No mistakes will be made if he approaches with honesty and generosity. He will have good fortune.

The marsh has flooded because the earth has reached the point of saturation. This is an extremely fortunate sign. A wise man may decide to give you his guidance. You will learn a great deal from his wisdom.

KUAN

Examine

HEXAGRAM 20

Examine. He washes his hands in preparation but has not yet made the sacrifice. He inspires confidence in others because of his dignified appearance.

Kuan combines wind and earth in the trigrams *Sun* and *K'un*. When the wind blows, plants and trees sway under its impact. The holy man's personality is like the wind, moulding people firmly into shape. *Kuan* can be likened to an important official who, knowing Heaven's way, keeps watch on the affairs of those below him. A man who understands Heaven's way will respect the natural laws which govern the earth. Just as the wind causes the grass to sway, a wise man inspires those who hear him. *Kuan* also stresses the need to prepare properly, signified by the washing of hands before sacrifice. In undertaking any venture, make sure you are in the proper frame of mind.

Line of Change

FIRST SIX

He looks at things like a boy. This behaviour is acceptable in lesser men but not in a superior man.

In this line you are like a child who tries to understand the world but of course cannot. You may not understand a wiser person's advice but nevertheless it will help you. Do not, however, try to understand too much – acknowledge your limits and remain within them. A wiser person should try to grasp more of what is being said as he has a responsibility to try harder.

SECOND SIX

He looks out of the door. This kind of behaviour is acceptable in a woman.

You are like a woman peering out through a crack in the door. Because you are looking from the dark into the light your vision is dimmed. You are like a woman without any education. Like a woman, you should follow the holy man's advice and study hard in order to understand more fully.

THIRD SIX

He examines his life so that he can decide whether to go forward or retreat.

You are like this line – in a weak position and yet having to move in one direction or another. Examination of your own thoughts and actions will help you judge yourself in relation to others.

FOURTH SIX

It is useful to be the king's guest since he can consider the achievements of the kingdom.

You should be like the wise official who, because he has studied the politics, morals and culture of many countries including his own, is able not only to advance himself but also help his country. Such a person who is well educated and aware of all that is going on will be given a position of responsibility. His decisions and actions should not be questioned or hindered.

FIFTH NINE

He examines his life. The wise man does not make mistakes.

An emperor should enlighten everyone – just like the sun. If you are in a top position you should examine all that you do to see how ordinary people are affected. If they are well then you are making the right decisions.

TOP NINE

He examines his character to see if he is wise. He will not lapse into error.

You should come to understand yourself first and then think about others and their problems. Do this and you will be acting wisely. Get rid of selfishness and you will not make any mistakes.

SHIH HO

Biting Through

HEXAGRAM 21

Biting through. Success. It is helpful to use the law.

The lower trigram is *Chen*, thunder, and the upper is *Li*, fire. When they combine they produce thunder and lightning. Their action is like a pair of lips which come together when eating. Excessive eating results in nothing more than gluttony, and excessive greed leads to corruption. This can only be controlled by harsh, often physical, punishment. In old China this might mean having your nose or ears cut off. This punishment must be given only by those who can judge properly and wisely.

Line of Change

FIRST NINE

His feet are trapped and his toes are cut off. There will be no mistakes.

You are like this yang line – bowed down by the weight of two yin lines on top. You are like a man who tries to put his large feet into shoes that are too small. Even if he squeezes his feet into them it means he is unable to walk properly. You should heed the saying 'A criminal can be tortured into abandoning his evil ways – but often all that is really needed is a severe warning.'

SECOND SIX

He sinks his teeth into tender flesh and bites off the nose. There will be no mistakes.

Be careful. This line is like a corrupt, greedy official. It is easy to tell right from wrong – as easy as biting into tender meat. However, anger, greed or frustration can cloud your

vision – just as the nose will disappear into the meat if you eat too quickly. You will suffer for your anger or greed.

THIRD SIX

He bites on tough meat and is poisoned. This is not a mistake but it is a cause for minor regrets.

Someone who starts to eat poisoned meat and then discovers the danger just in time is like someone who has taken bribes and then suddenly realizes that this is wrong. He returns the money. If you have done something shameful and of which you are embarrassed, do whatever has to be done to rectify the wrong.

FOURTH NINE

He bites on hard, bony meat. He receives the golden arrow. He will benefit from being firm and will recognize the dangers. There will be good fortune.

The difficulties ahead are represented by the hard, sinewy meat. The determination to overcome these and the rewards you will receive are symbolized by the straight golden arrow. Although times are tough, you will be in luck if you remain honest and careful.

FIFTH SIX

He discovers a small piece of gold when he bites on dried meat. He should be firm and recognize the dangers in order to avoid mistakes.

It is important that you remain sincere and impartial. Be as true and worthy as the Emperor. He helps everyone to live comfortably because of his wisdom and good behaviour.

TOP NINE

He is trapped in a wooden collar and has no ears. There will be bad fortune.

It is, of course, very distressing to be punished by having your freedom of movement curtailed. If you constantly seek after pleasure you will end up in disgrace. You will have trapped yourself by your own foolish behaviour.

PI

To Adorn

HEXAGRAM 22

To adorn. Success. There is little to be gained in giving him permission to undertake anything.

Pi contains the trigrams *Ken* and *Li*, mountain and fire. The mountain is green and pleasant but only becomes truly beautiful when flames from the earth light up its slopes. If you develop an appreciation of culture, this enhances the lives of everyone. A high official will be concerned with the education and wellbeing of all his people. The second, fourth and fifth lines of the *Pi* hexagram are yielding lines and are visibly prosperous, while the first, third and sixth lines are obstinate. The third line is the strongest of the hexagram and supports the rest.

Line of Change

FIRST NINE

He adorns his toes with finery. He steps out of the carriage and continues on foot.

While an ordinary person will try to keep his shoes clean by travelling by car, a wise man would rather travel by foot. This way he can act as a guide to others on the road. You may be like a beginner searching for the right way. You may need some help – symbolized here by the carriage – but it is better to try and progress by your own efforts.

SECOND SIX

He adorns his beard.

It is a mistake to lavish attention upon your beard – such a minor part of you – and to neglect the rest of your body.

This is like concentrating on some superfluous item and failing to care for your inner happiness.

THIRD NINE

His body is bejewelled as though he is sprinkled with dew. Constancy will bring good luck.

This yang line lies bewteen two yin lines and is like a handsome young man standing between two beautiful women. He can either be virtuous or immoral. So it is with you. You must, however, be virtuous. It is easy to succumb to temptation but you should remain honest and upright because, unless you do, your luck will disappear.

FOURTH SIX

His body is adorned so that he looks as though he is shining with light. He travels on a white, winged horse. He is not a thief but is looking for someone to marry.

You may be confused when tempted by pleasure and finery – but the right way to proceed will suddenly become clear. It is similar to when a man first approaches a woman. She may well be doubtful about him but nevertheless may wish to get to know him better. Once they are able to appreciate and understand each other, things will go well.

FIFTH SIX

His clothes and body are decorated with finery and he travels through hills and gardens. His roll of silk is poor and small. This may cause distress but in the end there will be good fortune.

The holy man says it is better to be cautious than extravagant. A simple unadorned life may embarrass you in certain circles, but you will know the true nature of your intentions.

TOP NINE

He is adorred only in white. There will be no mistakes.

An ostentatious lifestyle does not necessarily lead to a happy life. An artist may use all sorts of bright colours but yet fail to express his true feelings. He may need to return to a purer style or colour. In the same way you should also return to a simpler style of life.

PO

Peeling or Splitting

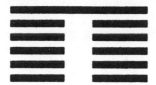

HEXAGRAM 23

Peeling or splitting. There is nothing to be gained by moving anywhere.

There are five yin lines in this hexagram about to overcome the one yang line so that they can convert it to a yin line. They are trying to undermine yang's power. The top trigram is *Ken*, the mountain, and the lower trigram is *K'un*, the earth. The mountain will eventually collapse since the earth is not strong enough to support it, just as the top line of the *Po* hexagram will disintegrate because of the weak yin lines. The world is in the grip of evil and it is a bad time for honest people. It is not wise to try to overthrow the evil ones at this time. Bide your time and let evil run its course. Use this time to plan for the future.

Line of Change

FIRST SIX

He breaks the leg of the bed. It is bad to destroy anything which is good.

This signifies a time of decay and collapse. It is like lying on a bed which has a rotten leg. If your thoughts are evil or impure you are heading for trouble.

SECOND SIX

He breaks the frame of the bed. It is bad to destroy things which are good and useful.

This weak yin line looks to the fifth line for help – but in vain as the fifth line is also yin. This is a time of increasing difficulty and you have little support – rather as though you were lying on a broken bed.

THIRD SIX

He is the one who breaks things. This is not a mistake.

The third line turns to Top Nine for help. This is the right time for you to break away from bad company and to join up with honest friends.

FOURTH SIX

He breaks both the bed and the skin. This is bad.

The bed is collapsing and unless you get up you will be hurt. Take care. This is a dangerous time. The holy man advises you not to be afraid to show your independence.

FIFTH SIX

He is kind to the people of the palace, treating them like a shoal of fish. There are many advantages in this.

The top yin line comes under the protection and guidance of the top yang line. In turn the top yin line leads the other yin lines. Rest assured. The time of decay and destruction is coming to an end.

TOP NINE

He is like a ripe fruit ready to be eaten. The wise man travels in a special carriage. A lesser man's home breaks up.

Anything which uses up all its resources must change. That is the way of the *I Ching*. You can be like the yang line, able to renew your energy after a difficult time. For instance, if all but one apple on a tree have been destroyed by worms, the one remaining apple still gives hope for a new apple tree. The wicked have left themselves without even a shelter. The wise man can now arise and, like the warmth of the sun, revitalize everyone.

FU

Return

HEXAGRAM 24

Return. Success. The man travelling to and fro will not be disrupted. His friends come to him and there is nothing wrong with this. It is in his way to come and go. He returns on the seventh day. It is helpful to have a place to stay, wherever that may be.

This hexagram follows the development of the previous one and means a return to normality after a period of decay and disintegration. Heaven operates in cycles so that there are good and bad times which arise and then pass away. A good person will always pull through these unfortunate times. The cycle runs for ever, because Heaven's way and man's way are the same. In the previous hexagram the six lines were stripped away. The seventh day is the day of rest, and after that the next six lines are like a new week – a fresh start. The yang line which is at the bottom of the *Fu* hexagram is a growth point and its influence rises upwards. Growth will occur naturally and gradually and the upper and lower trigrams, *K'un* and *Chen* will cooperate with each other. When everyone works together with the same intentions things turn out well.

Line of Change

FIRST NINE

He returns after travelling a short distance. There is nothing to regret. There will be very good fortune.

The yang line is beginning to grow and is the master line of this hexagram. When the *Po* hexagram has finished, it turns into the *Fu* hexagram. This is a good time. The wise man knows how to lead the people.

SECOND SIX

He returns resigned. There will be good fortune.

Be like this yin line – willing to accept help from the stronger yang line. Compare yourself with a newly married young woman who works harmoniously alongside her husband. Do not be proud or obstinate. If you have an open, charitable nature all will go well.

THIRD SIX

He returns many times. This is dangerous. There is no mistake.

There is danger. Always think carefully when planning any activity. Be careful.

FOURTH SIX

He starts out in the midst of others but returns alone.

You may have many friends, but if they are bad leave them. Listen to the advice of good friends. If you behave properly all will go well.

FIFTH SIX

He returns with dignity. There is no need for regret.

This is the Emperor's line. Be like it – solid as the earth and thus able to bear anything upon your back. Be kindhearted and faithful.

TOP SIX

He has been given misleading information about his return. This is bad. There will be misfortune and mistakes. If he summons the army to attack there will be a resounding defeat, which will also be disastrous for the country's ruler. It will not be possible to repell the invaders for another ten years.

Success can bring problems. Do not forget the dangers and deceits which lie in wait. The most fascinating events can capture your attention, but eventually you will have to return home to your normal life.

WU WANG

Not False

Not false. Great success. It is good to remain firm. He will be distressed if he is wild instead of upright. It is useless for him to try to go in any direction.

This hexagram is composed of the trigram *Chen*, thunder, at the bottom and *Ch'ien*, Heaven, on the top. Be careful, since this hexagram means unexpected events. It also means thinking about things you cannot possibly do. You might dream about pulling down the sky, but of course you cannot do it. The truly *Wu Wang* person does not think of things which are impossible. He is usually known for his honesty and truthfulness.

When people follow *Wu Wang*'s path everything works out well because *Wu Wang*'s way is both natural and just. If you know something is impossible do not trouble yourself over it. You are like a blind person who tries to do everything on his own and so makes mistakes. *Wu Wang* is naturally upright and honest. Someone who is not upright is like a man with eye trouble. He is upset because of this irritation and disasters follow because he is distracted. Someone who goes against Heaven's will does not receive Heaven's blessing, and disaster naturally follows.

Line of Change

FIRST NINE

He is sincere. Wherever he goes he will meet good fortune.

Although there is only one yang line in the lower trigram, it is the most important one. It is pure, like the mind of a young child. If you are well behaved and respectful everything will work out well. A young person who remains honest and respectful will be successful.

He does not plough the ground or clear the stable. But he still benefits from this wherever he goes.

You should do well the jobs you can do well. There is no great reward in this, but it should not trouble you. You will receive what is due. A wise man undertakes tasks because of their intrinsic value, not because of some future reward.

THIRD SIX

Even those who are truthful suffer misfortunes, like an ox which is tethered to a post and stolen by a passer-by. A local person suffers as a result of this misfortune.

This line spells trouble as it is not in the right place. This line means you are guilty of some crime in the past. One day this will catch up with you if you do not change. You must become more dependable and trustworthy.

FOURTH NINE

If he is able to stand firm there will be no mistakes.

You will not enjoy this situation – but accept it because Heaven has decreed it. Heaven knows that if you stand firm and true then all will be well.

FIFTH NINE

He is ill even though he is open and truthful. He does not use medicine. He will rejoice.

In this line you are like someone with a minor irritating illness. If you fuss around and call the doctor, then the illness will become serious. If you hit a problem which was not caused by you, ride it out rather than struggle and protest about it.

TOP NINE

He is not false yet if he tries to move he will be in difficulties. At this time it is wiser not to move.

This lines speaks of great strength and great obstinacy. By not thinking properly but simply trying to blunder on, you run the risk of disaster.

TA CH'U

Great Domesticating Powers

HEXAGRAM 26

Great powers of domestication. It is helpful to stand firm. He is lucky when he does not eat with his family. It is helpful to cross the great river.

A wise man accumulates knowledge and virtue and then shares this with the world. This is the meaning contained in the *Ta Ch'u* hexagram. You should build up material benefits which can then be used to everyone's benefit. What has been stored away must be shared, as long as you remember that wisdom as well as material goods are beneficial to all people.

The *Ta Ch'u* hexagram combines *Ken* and *Ch'ien*, mountain and heaven respectively. Since Heaven rests on the mountain this is a sign of treasures which have been hidden but which can be used to increase other people's knowledge. Things of the past can be useful in the present. The four strong yang lines are held back by the two weaker yin lines. Useful powers are being restrained so that they can be tended and nurtured in the hands of a wise ruler.

Ch'ien is in the lower part. *Ken* is on top. Ch'ien's nature is obstinate. The Top Nine is also determined, and looks like the sun shining from above. This is good. The Fifth Six is yin, yielding and like a queen. She accepts the help of many virtuous men. This hexagram is like a mountain with the sun shining on it and the rain falling. The mountain nourishes everything.

Line of Change

FIRST NINE

He is in a dangerous situation. It is wise to stop.

A young man often feels he must rush ahead with his plans. You must learn to slow down and thus avoid trouble.

SECOND NINE

The main strap underneath the carriage has been taken away.

The Second Nine needs the Fifth Six. Be like these two cooperating lines. It requires equal effort or contributions by partners to ensure all goes well.

THIRD NINE

He urges his good horse to travel on. It will be helpful to realize the dangers and behave accordingly. He trains daily in chariot driving and self-defence. There will be advantages in whatever direction he takes.

The holy man says you should not overdo things. Young people often go beyond their abilities because they think they understand everything. The real test will come if you show that you can manage your affairs properly over a period of time.

FOURTH SIX

The wild young bull is restrained by a yoke. There will be good fortune.

The bull represents two aspects of human behaviour. First, the young bull's new horns irritate him and he bangs his head against the wall. This shows that you must take care if you have new responsibilities. Second, a young bull is easily confused. It is therefore necessary to restrain such a creature, for its own good as well as for the sake of others. You should not take unnecessary risks. The best way to prevent this is to be aware of your limitations.

FIFTH SIX

The tusks of the gelded boar. There will be good fortune.

A boar's tusk can inflict a terrible wound. However, if you remove the aggressive impulse of the boar he is quite harmless. You should deal with dangerous situations by boldly tackling them at source.

TOP NINE

He is the one who controls the very substance of Heaven. There will be success.

This is a time of excellence and virtue. The world desperately needs this return to the Way of Heaven. There is no danger now, just prosperity and wellbeing.

I

Taking Nourishment

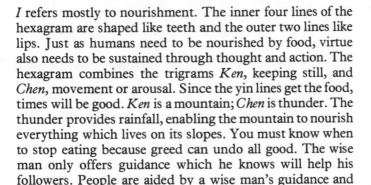

Taking nourishment. By behaving properly there will be good fortune. Look at what we are seeking to nourish. How people naturally seek nourishment.

I refers mostly to nourishment. The inner four lines of the hexagram are shaped like teeth and the outer two lines like lips. Just as humans need to be nourished by food, virtue also needs to be sustained through thought and action. The hexagram combines the trigrams *Ken*, keeping still, and *Chen*, movement or arousal. Since the yin lines get the food, times will be good. *Ken* is a mountain; *Chen* is thunder. The thunder provides rainfall, enabling the mountain to nourish everything which lives on its slopes. You must know when to stop eating because greed can undo all good. The wise man only offers guidance which he knows will help his followers. People are aided by a wise man's guidance and our bodies are nourished by careful eating and drinking. To keep healthy, eat good food. Do not be extravagant. Too much will harm your health. This is the main meaning of *I*.

Line of Change

FIRST NINE

Let your sacred tortoise go and look at me with your mouth open. There will be misfortunes.

You are behaving foolishly. You seem to think you are a sacred tortoise – able to exist on air alone. Yet you are in fact greedy and this is bad.

SECOND SIX

He turns everything upside down for nourishment. It goes

against the tradition of seeking nourishment above the ground. This will lead to evil.

You are acting like a miser. You have hoarded food yet pretend to be looking for nourishment. In the end others will seize what you have selfishly hoarded.

THIRD SIX

He rejects nourishment. This will be bad no matter how firm he is. He does nothing for ten years. This will not bring any disadvantages.

If you are always arrogant, pompous and extravagant you will have to work for years before you actually achieve anything of any significance.

FOURTH SIX

It is good if he turns things upside down for nourishment. Like a tiger who glares down, he is ready to drive them out. This is no mistake.

You may well be tough and vigorous but you need others to help you share the responsibilities. The importance of hunting out suitable colleagues can be likened to the sun's need for the moon in order to cast light upon the earth at night.

FIFTH SIX

He is opposed to the correct traditional teachings. He will have good fortune if he lives properly. He should not be allowed to try to cross the great river.

You can be compared to an official who, although unorthodox, needs the support of the top line or higher authority in order to carry out a certain task. Although you may not be strong you are honest and hardworking. Through the help of those above you you will succeed.

TOP NINE

The source of nourishment. It is dangerous but there will be good fortune. It is helpful to cross the great river.

The top line is the line of authority. If you really care about things everything will happen as promised. Now is the time to move forward.

TA KUO

Great Experience

HEXAGRAM 28

Great experience. The main support is weak. It is helpful to move in any direction. There will be success.

The four strong yang lines inside *Ta Kuo* exert great power but they are threatened by the hidden dangers of the two yin lines on the outside of the hexagram. The yin lines can neither give instructions nor help the strong yang lines. The yang lines are likened to a beam which is sturdy in the middle but weak at the edges: while the middle of the beam can support a strong weight the edges are under severe stress. The lower trigram is *Sun*, wind, which is gentle and prosperous, the upper trigram is *Tui*, the marsh, which is happy and content.

Line of Change

FIRST SIX

He puts white woven mats on the ground. There will be no mistakes.

Soft white straw mats are good to kneel on for those who wish to pray. You should make suitable preparation before you start new ventures.

SECOND NINE

The ageing willow sprouts new shoots. The old husband has married a young wife. There are no disadvantages.

The Second Nine is linked to the First Six. It is like an old tree putting forth a new vigorous shoot. You too can be invigorated and show new energy – just as an old man who marries a young woman discovers a fresh lease of life – as long as they are well matched.

THIRD NINE

The main support is weak. This is bad.

This hexagram is like a stout beam which has rotted at both ends. You should beware. You may be tough, but if difficulties arise which cause your friends to leave you then, like the beam, you will collapse.

FOURTH NINE

The main support has held. This is good fortune. Another support will only cause regret.

This is a good line. You should seek support from those above and below you who are of a common mind. Do this and nothing will defeat you.

FIFTH NINE

The aging willow flowers. The old wife marries a young husband. There will be mistakes and no praise.

Beware that you are not like the old aspen tree or the old woman. The flowers of the old tree are without fragrance. The marriage of an old woman will not produce children. Ensure your efforts are not equally fruitless. Look to what and how you do things, even if you feel that currently you are not doing anything wrong.

TOP SIX

He crosses the stream and the water rises above his head. This is bad, but there are no mistakes or blame.

This line is out on a limb and thus dangerous. It has no particular skills and is difficult to control. There are many changes facing you because you are overstretched. However, you will get through if you behave sensibly.

K'AN

The Watery Depths

HEXAGRAM 29

The watery depths are twofold. Have faith. He keeps his heart faithful and prospers. Whatever he does is worthwhile.

The two yang lines are enclosed by yin lines and are in danger unless they can keep the confidence and determination needed to find their way through. The *K'an* hexagram is made up of two *K'an* trigrams, which mean water. The yang lines are like two rivers which lie at the base of a deep ravine. The water continues to flow along its natural course with no beginning or end in sight. A wise man will not avoid the dangers which lie ahead but will confront them with patience and understanding and his knowledge, like the waters, will not dry up.

Line of Change

FIRST SIX

The waters are twofold. The man enters the watery cavern. This is evil.

It is easy to get out of your depth when you take on something new. At such a time you can be misled. This is a time of danger. Beware of bad influences.

SECOND NINE

The watery depths are dangerous. His desires will not be fully satisfied.

Be very careful. You are like the Fifth Nine, lying between the two yin lines and thus at risk. Keep calm, and although you will not achieve much you will be all right.

THIRD SIX

He is confronted by the watery depths whether he goes forward or retreats. When danger such as this is around he should stop and rest, otherwise he will fall into the watery depths. Do nothing.

The third line indicates danger whether you move backwards or forwards. Action without proper forethought will result in disaster. This is an extremely dangerous situation so do not expect any good to come out of it.

FOURTH SIX

He only has a bottle of wine and a basket of rice and he uses ordinary earthenware pots. He has agreed to bring enlightenment. There is nothing wrong in this.

In times of crisis a good official will set a good example by practising economy. Things are in a bad way. Like the official who only has one cup of wine and two dishes for his main meal, you should set a good example. Difficult times call for stringent measures. There is nothing to be ashamed of in adopting a simple lifestyle if by doing so you can help restore the situation.

FIFTH NINE

The watery depths are not overflowing. Order is approaching. There will be no mistakes.

This is the Emperor's position and means you have reached safety after a time of difficulty. However, you are also, like this line, surrounded by those who are weak. When danger appears choose the least difficult path. Do not try to do great things. Be grateful that you are safe.

TOP SIX

He is bound with thick, strong ropes and imprisoned behind walls of thorn bushes. For three years he cannot find a means of escape. This is evil.

You are greatly constrained and thus cannot escape. This is a dangerous position to be in. If you behave properly and remain faithful, you will survive, no matter how tough things become.

LI

To Shine Brightly, to Part

HEXAGRAM 30

To part. Is is useful to stand firm and behave well. This will bring success. Take care of the cows. There will be good fortune.

The trigram *Li*, fire, appears twice in this hexagram. It stands both for illumination and for civilization. *Li* can be harmful or beneficial depending on how we use its power. The two yang lines in each trigram illuminate the yin lines; the yin lines in their turn cling to the radiant yang lines. All people and creatures need the support of Heaven and earth for their survival. For example, we provide fodder for cows, who then plough the fields so that we can plant crops. This then nourishes the young cows and they provide us with milk. This dependence upon nature's way is essential for the continuance of life.

The sun is represented in both the *Li* trigams. The sun illuminates the earth during the day and at night the moon reflects the sun's light onto the earth. This is why the trigram *Li* occurs twice in the *Li* hexagram.

Line of Change

FIRST NINE

He moves but in a very confused way. If this is done with good and proper intentions there will be no mistakes.

When about to start some new task, think carefully about all the various factors involved. Rid yourself of all those who mislead you and concentrate instead on those who are helpful. Do not rush into a new project without first giving it thorough consideration.

SECOND SIX

The yellow parts. There will be good fortune.

Yellow refers to the sun at midday. It is also the Imperial colour, a sign of nobility and culture. You are entering a time of good fortune.

THIRD NINE

The setting sun shines as it goes down. The old sing and beat their pots, or complain about their lot. This is evil.

The evening sun is setting and darkness will soon be upon us. Remember life's span is short. This is particularly so if you waste your younger years in self-indulgence.

FOURTH NINE

It comes unexpectedly. It is like a fire which dies down and is discarded.

This line is set betwixt fires. It shows you as being like an incompetent official who, beset by problems, makes one last attempt to solve them, fails and collapses. Soon even his name is forgotten. If you will be patient you will find that turning to your superiors will help you overcome such difficulties.

FIFTH SIX

He leaves in floods of tears, crying and bemoaning. There will be good fortune.

You are like a good emperor who weeps because he does not have good officials. Like him you fear for those under you. However, hold back the tears; eventually the troubles will pass and all will be well.

TOP NINE

The king uses him to attack. Skilfully he kills the leaders but spares the followers. This is not a mistake.

Cultivate your good characteristics and eradicate the bad. It is like dealing with a rebellion. Root out the bad influences, as you would execute the leaders of a rebellion. But do not destroy that which is potentially good in you, just as you would not kill all those who had been caught up in a rebellion.

HSIEN

All-Embracing

All-embracing. It is helpful to stand firm and behave properly. Marriage to a young woman will be fortunate.

Hsien combines *Tui* and *Ken*, the marsh resting on the mountain. The marsh's moisture nourishes the mountain slopes and makes the land fertile. In the same way the love of a man and a woman culminates in the union of marriage.

The yang line in the lower trigram is determined and steady, whereas the yin line in the upper trigram is flexible and accommodating. This particular combination is a good foundation for successful partnerships. The mountain and the marsh are interdependent; the mountain needs the marsh for its moisture as much as the marsh needs to rest upon the mountain. A wise man instructs those who come to him but he also listens to the good advice offered by others and thus develops good relationships from which all may benefit.

Line of Change

FIRST SIX

He concentrates on wriggling his toes.

The toe is a useful but not very impressive part of the body. Do not be like the man who spends his time worrying about his toes. Do not expend all your energy on minor matters. If you have a lowly position, make sure you do your work well, even if you feel that no one notices you.

SECOND SIX

He concentrates on the calves of his legs. This is evil. If he stays where he is there will be good fortune.

You are like the calves of the leg. You are taken wherever the rest wish to take you. If you do what is right in your job you will be all right, but beware of being carried away by sudden impulses.

THIRD NINE

He concentrates on flexing his thigh muscles. He follows others closely. Going forward in this way will bring unhappiness.

The top of the leg is used to depict the sort of control you should have over your emotions. Be calm and patient. Do not go rushing off after people. It will do you no good.

FOURTH NINE

By being firm and righteous there will be good fortune. This prevents regret. If he is restless, moving to and fro, only his friends will take him seriously.

Fourth Nine stresses how important careful thought and reflection are. An unsteady or disturbed mind leads to confused actions and will bring little in the way of success.

FIFTH NINE

He concentrates on the back of his neck. There will be no regret.

The neck is the stiffest part of the body and remains firm no matter how we use our bodies. If you have a strong will and a clear mind you can be open to external influences. Because you know what is right you will not be misled or confused by such influences.

TOP SIX

He concentrates on his jaw and tongue.

Sweet words are usually dishonest words. It is foolish to try to influence people by using meaningless or flattering phrases.

HENG

Constant

HEXAGRAM 32

Constant. There will be success. There is no mistake. It is helpful to stand firm and behave righteously. It is helpful to go forward in any direction.

The *Heng* hexagram combines *Chen* and *Sun*, thunder and wind, which also represent an elder son and daughter respectively. Thunder is the powerful force, and wind the gentle force resting underneath. When the thunder claps, the wind follows in its trail; it is just like a wife after marriage following her husband wherever he goes. No mistakes will be made when things follow a proper course. *Heng* is durable and strong-minded like the sun and the moon, which are eternally in the sky and ceaselessly illuminate the earth. Thunder and lightning may suddenly appear and subside but they endure for ever. This is like a wise man who understands how his life is guided and through this understands the law by which all things exist and persist.

Line of Change

FIRST SIX

Too great an emphasis on constancy will bring evil, even though he behaves firmly and righteously. Nothing at all can be gained here.

Have patience and do not expect immediate success. Work step by step. Deal with everything gradually and carefully. By wanting too much too quickly you will end up empty-handed.

SECOND NINE

All regret is removed.

You should be like this line, able both to stand firm and yet also to change when necessary. Although you may want to try to do something rather difficult, hold back and thus avoid any mistakes.

THIRD NINE

He does not always make use of virtue. Others think of this as a disgrace. Even if he behaves properly there will be mistakes.

Your virtue shows itself in both thought and deed. Make sure you are to be trusted in both. If you are not, then you can expect failure, shame and regret.

FOURTH NINE

There is no game in the field.

The hunter who searches for game in deserted areas could wait for ever without firing a single shot. Look in the right places or your efforts will be in vain.

FIFTH SIX

By righteous behaviour he increases his virtue. This is good for the wife but bad for the husband.

A wife should always abide by her husband's decisions. If the reverse happens the marriage will be a disaster. Be a good husband, always aware of what is going on, otherwise you and your family will suffer because of your ignorance.

TOP SIX

He constantly excites himself. This is evil.

Heng means constancy and endurance. Do not overdo things. There have to be calmer moments in life so that you can see the pattern which events are following. Constant haste and restlessness are likely to bring disaster.

TUN

To hide

HEXAGRAM 33

To hide. There will be success. There is a small advantage to be gained from being firm and behaving properly.

Tun means to 'hide away' or 'conceal'. When we are governed by foolish leaders, wise men cannot be found. They are not hiding for fear of challenging corrupt authority but because they are planning the best course of action for social change. The *Tun* hexagram combines *Ch'ien* and *Ken*, Heaven and mountain. This is a time for withdrawal and consideration, not for action. The two yin lines at the bottom seem to be giving trouble to the officials at the top. They seem to sense that it is too dangerous to move at this time. The best plan is for you to temporarily withdraw so as not to get caught up in either the corruption or the violence.

Line of Change

FIRST SIX

It is dangerous because the tail is hidden. Do not try to move.

Do not procrastinate over important matters otherwise you will end up at the tail end of actions or plans. If you are confused or in danger do not attempt anything new. Bide your time and all will be well.

SECOND SIX

He grasps it tightly, using an ox's yellow hide. He cannot be persuaded to let go.

Put your trust in a courageous and respected man. A good man sets an example for everyone. He will behave like a leader who stays with his people when his town is attacked.

THIRD NINE

He hides away as though he is bound to this place. He is ill and troubled. Keeping domestic servants or a concubine will bring good fortune.

You are confused and bewildered because you have been tricked, and you are upset. Be patient. Everything will settle down if you avoid making others jealous.

FOURTH NINE

He hides away well. This is fortunate for a wise man. It is impossible for a lesser man.

Do not abuse your authority. Keep alert so that you can recognize the right time for withholding action or comment. Do not be like a weak man who is not considerate and who misuses his authority. He easily makes mistakes which he later regrets.

FIFTH NINE

He hides himself away very carefully. Righteous behaviour will bring good fortune.

You must be like this line, which is honest and accommodating. If you have worked hard feel free to rest. You deserve a comfortable life because you have done so much for others.

TOP NINE

He hides away honourably. This will bring many advantages.

You have nothing to worry about because you are polite, honest and considerate. Like this line, you are in an unchallenged position. You will have a comfortable life.

TA CHUANG

Great Strength

HEXAGRAM 34

Great strength. It is helpful to act properly and firmly.

The *Ta Chuang* hexagram is the reverse of the previous hexagram. It is strong and powerful. Weaker people have now retreated into the background and wise leaders have come to the fore. This hexagram combines *Chen* and *Ch'ien*, thunder and Heaven. The yang lines in the four lower positions are accumulating power and, given the opportunity, they could become too powerful. In this hexagram they must contain their strength and behave correctly. *Chen*, thunder, has strength and energy and is in harmony with Heaven. The thunder can be likened to a powerful leader who can only maintain his position of respect as long as he is just and considerate and so establishes a harmonious government. A wise man must be of good character and reasonable. Confucius said to Ngan Chi, 'Without politeness, do not look; without politeness, do not hear; without politeness, do not speak; without politeness, do not act.'

Line of Change

FIRST NINE

His strength lies in his toes. It is certainly a bad time to attack.

At the moment your position can be compared to a big toe. Although you want to demonstrate your abilities, nobody will take any notice.

SECOND NINE

We will be fortunate if he behaves properly.

Prove that you can do your job well by being disciplined and persevering. You will get excellent results.

The small man uses all his strength, whereas the wise man does not do this. There is grave danger even when he behaves properly. He is like a ram who butts a fence and only succeeds in trapping his horns.

Do not be like a ram which lowers its horns and blindly charges at a gate. He may be the strongest animal in his flock but nevertheless he will be easily injured. Always behave according to your position. Be wise and observant, otherwise you will be the cause of your own downfall.

FOURTH NINE

Righteous conduct will bring good fortune and remorse will disappear. He approaches a fence determined not to get trapped. His strength is like the strength of a heavy wagon's wheels.

Like this yang line, you can be very obstinate. Use your stubbornness wisely and you will be powerful. An obstinate nature is like a car brake which is hidden and yet, at a touch, regulates the car's speed. You may look weak but have great inner strength.

FIFTH SIX

He changes and loses his ram-like nature. There is nothing to regret.

Your stubborn behaviour could lead you into trouble. Do not be like a ram who mindlessly charges through the gates of the field. Like the ram, you could get lost because of one thoughtless action.

TOP SIX

He is like a ram butting a fence. He cannot retreat or advance. He cannot gain anything by carrying on like this. If he understands the dangers there will be good fortune.

Do not try to exceed your own capabilities because you will only cause yourself difficulties. A ram who charges at a fence will trap his horns in the wire; in the same way you must not rush blindly into difficult projects. Take your time. Be calm, work hard and everything will find the right course.

CHIN

To Advance

To advance. The vigorous noble. He uses his charm like a display of fine horses. Three times within the space of one day he is received in audience.

The *Chin* hexagram combines *Li* and *K'un*, fire and earth. The sun is unhindered as it rises above the earth, reaching its peak at noon, and everything upon earth benefits from its goodness. The goodness in human nature can be obscured by greed and hatred just as the sun's reflection in a mirror can be obscured by dust. The text is illustrated by the story of an emperor who rewards one of his lords with several horses, and as a result this lord works even harder in support of the emperor. The people are loyal to the emperor because he is wise and in return he accepts the responsibilities of government. He is like a horse who is willing to carry a man great distances because he is obedient and the man cares for him.

Line of Change

FIRST SIX

He seems to advance and retreat at the same time. If he behaves properly all will work out well. If confidence is expressed remain calm. There will be no mistakes.

Do not fret if you think you have been forgotten by your friends. Do not feel downhearted or angry if you think no one pays attention to your work. Be calm and hardworking. Everything will work out well.

SECOND SIX

He appears to advance, but at the same time he is sad. If he behaves properly he will receive very good fortune from his heavenly mother.

Because of a sycophantic colleague you find yourself cut off from those above. Do not worry, a good leader is never fooled by flattery. If you are always running into obstacles, do not despair. Keep going because in the end your hard work will be rewarded.

THIRD SIX

Everyone is in harmony. All regret has disappeared.

You are gradually making progress. Although someone may try to block your path others will come to your help. By working hard and being honest, people will come to see your true value.

FOURTH NINE

He is like a hamster when he advances. He is in danger even if he behaves properly.

Do not be like a corrupt official who misuses his position of authority. You will not get away with this sort of behaviour. It is dangerous and will soon be discovered.

FIFTH SIX

All regrets have now gone. Do not be worried by what is gained or lost. To advance will bring good fortune and many advantages.

A wise queen is constantly aware of corrupt officials. You must be like her, selfishly working for the good of others. Everything you want will come to you eventually.

TOP NINE

He advances with his horns. He only uses them to punish the city. There will be good fortune. There is no mistake. Even if he behaves properly there will be problems.

You are working towards a goal. Do not be obstinate. You can reach this goal if you are thoughtful and open.

MING I

Brightness Dimmed

Brightness dimmed. It is wise to appreciate the dangers and behave properly.

The sun is setting in the *Ming I* hexagram and conditions become dark and dangerous. *Ming I* is the reverse of *Chin* because a corrupt and devious leader has taken over authority. The upper trigram is *K'un*, the earth, and the lower is *Li*, fire. *Li*'s light has been overshadowed by the earth, and although trapped it still holds on to its beauty and clarity. When you are caught up in difficult and dangerous circumstances do not allow yourself to be swept along with events. Be patient and the right time will come. You may have to appear outwardly compromising, but ensure that in your heart you are true. All may seem dark, but fear not – the light is coming.

Line of Change

FIRST NINE

The brightness is dimmed with flying and he lowers his wings. The wise man goes away and does not eat for three days. Wherever he travels people speak of him unkindly.

This is an unlucky time. Keep well away from corruption even if you have to suffer for your beliefs. The Chinese say, 'It is better not to eat for three days than to eat in the dark.'

SECOND SIX

Brightness is dimmed. He is wounded in the left thigh. He uses a swift horse to save himself. There will be good fortune.

This time is right to sort out your difficulties. Be honest and dependable and all will be well.

While hunting in the south the brightness is dimmed. He captures the most important general. He should not be too hasty when he tries to restore order.

Do not expect to wipe out corruption with one blow. Keep your plans secret so that the others cannot ruin them. You may feel like an honest official who cannot rid the town of corruption because those above him are all involved. Act very carefully.

FOURTH SIX

He enters the left side of the belly. He reaches the heart of that which dims the brightness. He leaves through the courtyard gate.

You have come to know from personal experience whether a situation is beyond improvement. An official who works closely alongside the king will soon be aware of extensive corruption within the palace. Since he is not actually a member of the royal family he can always leave when he wants to. Like the official, you must make a hasty exit when you sense danger.

FIFTH SIX

Wherever brightness is dimmed, be like Prince Chi. It is good to behave properly.

The safety of a country is not solely dependent upon an emperor. You and those around you must choose wise men to govern.

TOP SIX

No light, just obscurity. First of all he climbs to Heaven. Afterwards he returns to earth.

If you lack intelligence do not expect to hold power for long. You simply will not have the foresight to plan sensibly for the future.

CHIA JEN

The Family

HEXAGRAM 37

The family. It is good if a woman behaves properly.

The *Chia Jen* hexagram means family organization and structure. The upper trigram, *Sun*, and the lower trigram, *Li*, are wind and fire respectively, and represent the difference between indoors and outdoors. The second line represents a gentle and understanding wife who takes charge of the household affairs; while the fifth line refers to a husband who takes on the responsibility of affairs outside the home. The second line respects line five and together they have a harmonious and prosperous relationship. A husband must accept the role of supporter and provider and a wife must take responsibility for her children's education.

The holy man stressed the importance of a good woman for a successful family life. A healthy family is not totally dependent upon the husband and wife but also needs trust and hard work from each family member. These family relationships are reflected within the hexagram itself. The family unit provides a firm foundation for a country and is a source of guidance for other people.

Line of Change

FIRST NINE

He has restrictions in his family. Regrets will disappear.

How do you run things? Do not be weak. For instance, a woman should not allow her husband complete control over the family. On the other hand, a husband should be watchful of his wife's behaviour. Do not spoil your children because they will not respect you. Structure your family sensibly and all will be well.

SECOND SIX

She should not follow her own desires. She should be at the centre of the home preparing food. Her good conduct brings great fortune.

An ideal wife should focus her attention on the needs of her home, family and husband. Like a wife, manage your home affairs wisely and your work will prosper.

THIRD NINE

Excessive severity in the family brings repentance and dangers. There is also good fortune. If the women and children are always chattering this will end in distress and humiliation.

Do not be too harsh nor too soft. Too much discipline in your home will cause argument. Being too soft, however, will result in a loss of your authority. Find a delicate balance between discipline and leniency.

FOURTH SIX

The wealthy family. There is extremely good fortune.

The happiness of the home is dependent on your wife's character. A wise, honest and dedicated woman creates a harmonious, prosperous and stable family. Be like this in your dealings with those who are closest to you.

FIFTH NINE

The Emperor is very forgiving with his family. There is nothing to worry about. There will be good fortune.

Be like a good ruler. He must be open-minded and true. Guide those around you with the same devotion and love with which a father guides his family.

TOP NINE

He is confident and has a regal presence. There will be good fortune in the end.

If you are the head of a family, always set a good example. Even when the time comes to hand over authority to your eldest son, you must still set an example. You should be trusted and respected. Behave accordingly.

K'UEI

Opposition

HEXAGRAM 38

Opposition. There will be good fortune in minor matters.

The *K'uei* hexagram combines a fire nature and a marsh nature in its upper and lower trigrams, *Li* and *Tui*. The fire and marsh are travelling in opposite directions to each other, the fire flames up while the marsh seeps down. *Li* also represents an elder daughter and *Tui* a younger daughter. A time will come when the two girls marry and grow apart from each other, since their allegiance will lie with their husbands. They will be unable to do any great projects together but are still close enough to deal with minor problems.

 The fire which is contained in the hexagram illuminates the earth and the marsh provides moisture for the earth. They both provide nourishment so although their actions are opposite their effect is the same. This can be compared to higher and lower officials. Their roles are different but their aim is the same.

Line of Change

FIRST NINE

There is no need for repentance. He has lost his horse but does not go in search of it because it will return of its own accord. If he meets evil men he should avoid making any mistakes.

Although lines one and four are yang they are not well matched. One is patient and the other is scheming. Likewise there will be times when your life does not run smoothly. When separation or opposition crops up do not try to alter this. When a horse bolts it will return of its own accord just as the troubles in your life will eventually fade away.

By chance he meets his lord in a narrow street. He does not make any mistakes.

This is a difficult time to meet other people because the Second Nine and the Fifth Six are in the wrong positions. However, when you do get the chance to meet others you will form inseparable friendships.

THIRD SIX

The wagon is seen as it is dragged backwards. His oxen are obstructed. The man's own hair and nose are cut off. This is not a good start, but the end will be better.

You may be forced to leave others whom you know well for a while. This is just like lines three and six which are forced apart by lines two and four. Any doubts that you may have about a friend are displaced. Your friendship will be renewed, like a husband who returns to his wife when his suspicion of her infidelity is proved to be groundless.

FOURTH NINE

Alone in opposition. He can be confident when he meets the top man. There is danger but there will be no mistakes.

At the moment you may feel isolated from others. Give yourself time to understand people. With the help of a wise man you will develop a long-lasting friendship.

FIFTH SIX

There is no need for repentance. His own relative bites through the covering. Where is the fault in carrying on like this?

If cousins have not seen each other for years they will be ecstatic when they meet.

TOP NINE

Alone in opposition. He can see the pig carrying all the filth on its back. There is a carriage full of ghosts. At first the bow is drawn, then it is unstrung. He is not a robber in the act of theft, but a bridegroom going to woo. If he carries on along this way he will encounter rain and there will be good fortune.

Deal calmly with any fears which are troubling you. A quiet, calm approach will clear away your worries just as the sky clears after a rainstorm.

CHIEN

Obstruction

There are advantages in the southwest. There are no advantages in the northeast. It is helpful to see the great man. Behave properly and there will be good fortune.

The *Chien* hexagram combines water and mountain in the trigrams *K'an* and *Ken*. A man who attempts to climb a mountain and then cross water is presented with serious but not impossible difficulties. The *Chien* hexagram instructs us to move slowly, gaining experience as we go. Eventually enough strength and determination will be gained to face such risks and overcome obstructions. You should be well aware of the dangers which lie in wait, but should not deliberate for too long as to which direction you take. The hexagram tells how Wen Wang was imprisoned in Li, with only two possible routes of escape, the southwest, which, if he crossed the Yellow River, was a safe area, and the northeast, which was dogged by dangers and obstacles. Retreat to the southwest area was his immediate choice, but this was only as a temporary measure while he decided how to cope with the risks ahead. The southwest is *K'an*'s direction, and since *K'an* is yielding and patient you will eventually receive help. The northeast is *Ken*'s direction and is blocked by icy mountains.

Line of Change

FIRST SIX

The way ahead is blocked. Returning will bring praise.

You are inexperienced, like this yang line. You are faced with serious risks but cannot rely on others. Bide your time. Wait for the right moment before you do anything.

SECOND SIX

The king's servant faces many obstructions and difficulties. He is not to be blamed.

You are honest and willing to help others but your actions are curtailed by another person. You are faced with certain risks which you cannot avoid or control. Deal with these directly.

THIRD NINE

To go forward is to encounter difficulties. The reverse of this is to return.

These are dangerous times; stay close to others. Be like King Wen who returned to his people rather than rush headlong into danger. Although you have enough courage to cope with danger, remember your responsibilities. Give yourself time to think through the situation carefully.

FOURTH SIX

To go forward is to encounter obstacles. By returning he is united.

This is not the right time to struggle single-handedly. Gather around you a group of clever and supportive friends so that they can help you overcome any difficulties.

FIFTH NINE

There are very great obstacles. His friends come back to him.

Although King Wen was imprisoned for his beliefs, two thirds of the country rallied to his help. Because others respect and trust you, you too can rely on their help when you are in great trouble.

TOP SIX

To go forward is to encounter obstacles. It is better if he turns back. There will be good fortune. It is helpful to see the great man.

Although your plans are in danger you must nevertheless be determined enough to carry them through. Seek help from someone whom you trust and who is strong-minded.

HSIEH

Let Loose

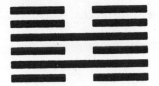

HEXAGRAM 40

Let loose. There are advantages in the southwest. If there is nothing else to be done there is good fortune in his returning. If he has to go anywhere it will be more fortunate to travel early.

The *Hsieh* hexagram is in a reverse position to the previous hexagram. The trigram *Chen*, thunder, is on top and *K'an*, water, is below. Although *Chen* is riding on *K'an*'s danger it also has enough power of movement to escape. This hexagram can be likened to a sky heavy with clouds, a warning of a thunderstorm. After the thunder and rain the clouds part and the sky is once more brilliantly clear. This is the time for deliverance from danger and safe return to familiar people and places.

Line of Change

FIRST SIX

There will be no mistakes.

You are ready and willing to work with others, just as the First Six is now willing to work with the obstinate Fourth Nine.

SECOND NINE

He catches three foxes in a field. He receives the yellow arrow. Proper behaviour brings good fortune.

This line is like an official who is rewarded by the Fifth Six because he has killed three foxes in a hunt. You too will be rewarded when you take on responsibility. Use your authority wisely.

THIRD SIX

The man is carrying a burden on his back. He is also travelling in a carriage and this will lead to robbers attacking him. No matter how properly he behaves there will be sadness.

Do not live above your means. This line is like a man who carefully guards the valuables kept in his car. In order to make them more secure he straps them to his back and thereby attracts thieves. He has the added difficulty of driving the car. Take care of your goods. Lead your life modestly.

FOURTH NINE

Free yourself from your toe. Then your trusted friends will come to you.

Do not overestimate your capabilities. This line is like a thumb which tries to iron out major problems without help from the other fingers. You may be capable but you need trusting friends in difficult times.

FIFTH SIX

The wise man removes the carriage and has good fortune. He has the confidence of a lesser man.

This line is like a queen who, because of her good leadership and inspiring character, has saved her country from ruin. If you are strong and kind you can sort out any difficulties and, like the queen, inspire acquaintances who have become selfish or dissatisfied.

TOP SIX

The lord fires an arrow at a falcon which is perched on the top of a wall. He hits it. This act brings advantages for him.

Do not despair. When the situation seems hopeless outsiders will come to your help, just as this weak line has been rescued by the Fourth Nine.

SUN

Injured

HEXAGRAM 41

Injured. Have confidence. Supreme good fortune and no regrets. Proper behaviour is possible. It is good to advance when fully prepared. Two baskets of offerings may be better than offerings which are expensive.

This hexagram combines *Tui*, the marsh, and *Ken*, the mountain. When the water in the marsh, which rests at the bottom of the mountain, evaporates the mountain benefits as the evaporating water nourishes its slopes. It then rises to form clouds which turn to rain, eventually falling back to the lake. The hexagram illustrates the shifting patterns of wealth which are possible without making the government or the people suffer. Increases and decreases in fortune are not necessarily detrimental. If you pay your taxes you are poorer and the government is richer, but you will receive it back. Because changes in fortune do vary it is important to save money while you can so you can deal better with these shifts in wealth.

Line of Change

FIRST NINE

He leaves his own work. He goes to help another person. There is no cause for regret if he deliberates on what he is doing.

Be like this strong First Nine which has come to the help of the weaker Fourth Six. Complete your own work but at the same time show your generosity by quickly and quietly helping others.

It is good to behave properly and to attack evil. It is not possible to help another without helping himself.

This is the main position of the lower hexagram. This line ought to be helpful but in this hexagram it is too obstinate to do anything. If you attempt to help others you must take care. Your offers may be thrown back in your face.

THIRD SIX

Three men travel together, but one then disagrees with the others and he therefore goes. He then finds another person as a companion.

This line refers to the eternal triangle of love. Two people can be content together but a third arouses jealousy. If you are single you can find a suitable partner.

FOURTH SIX

He tackles his weakness and is then able to help others. This is good. He has nothing to regret by doing this.

This weak line needs the First Nine's help. In the same way you must rely on friends when you are ill. With their help you will make a speedy recovery.

FIFTH SIX

He may receive advantages because friends give him ten tortoise shells. They will not accept them back. There will be very great fortune.

This is the Emperor's line. It is wealthy because it is supported wholeheartedly by the Second Nine. If you follow Heaven's way you will naturally be blessed.

TOP NINE

He does not injure. He has the advantage and there is no cause for remorse. It is good to remain firm and true because good fortune will naturally arise. He has the advantage in every move. He draws to himself able ministers, not just relatives.

If you are unselfish and hard-working not only will you be personally pleased and rewarded, but you will also affect everyone whom you meet.

I

Increase

HEXAGRAM 42

Increase. It is helpful to go forward with plans in mind. It is good to cross the great river.

The *Sun* hexagram has been turned upside down to become the *I* hexagram which combines thunder and wind in the trigram *Chen* and *Sun*. When the thunder rolls and the wind howls they strengthen each other and benefit everything else in the world. The Fifth Nine and the Second Six are in the correct position in charge of the upper and lower trigrams respectively. The joint movement of the thunder and the wind brings prosperity. This is a good time for business expansion which will benefit the country and its people.

A wise man understands the importance of serving and guiding others, and if he is responsible for a mistake he will correct it at once, just as a typhoon stops when the thunder rolls. By giving himself to the service of others he has helped the community. A good leader's words and actions nourish his followers in the same way that Heaven sends the rain which makes the earth fruitful.

Line of Change

FIRST NINE

It is good to undertake impressive actions. There will be great fortune and nothing to regret.

You are inexperienced like this first line which is helped by the wise Fourth Six. When an experienced person offers help use it well. You will be fortunate.

SECOND SIX

Someone gives him the advantage by giving him ten pairs of tortoise shells. These cannot be resisted. He will always be fortunate as long as he behaves properly. The king who offers what he receives to the supreme ruler will be very fortunate.

You will always be lucky if you are trustworthy, loving and modest. You will be well rewarded, like the Second Six which has been given the full support of the Emperor's line, the Fifth Nine.

THIRD SIX

He gains advantage by using evil. There is nothing wrong in this. He has confidence. He walks the straight path and, using the seal, announces himself to the prince.

Be sensible. You can prevent a crisis if you ask an experienced person for help.

FOURTH SIX

He walks the true path. He announces himself to the prince who will follow. It is good to be relied upon, even to the extent of helping to remove the capital.

If an important decision has to be made and there are two groups, each arguing their case, choose someone who is honest and impartial as mediator. His advice can be put to good use.

FIFTH NINE

He is confident in his generosity and kindness. There will be great fortune in not speaking or asking. He can be confident because he will recognize his virtue and kindness.

You must be like a wise emperor who acts for the good of his people and in return receives their respect. Your actions should never be prompted by thoughts of a possible reward. Genuine kindness and consideration should come naturally.

TOP NINE

He is of no benefit to anyone. Someone may even hit him. He sets no standard for his attitudes and this is evil.

Only ask for what is due to you. Although this hexagram means increase, do not let others think you are grasping or greedy.

KUAI

New Outcome

HEXAGRAM 43

New outcome. He must display it in the king's court. He must speak confidently with strict regard to honesty. There is danger. It is not a good idea to tell the city, nor is it useful to rush to arms. It is helpful to carry on with plans already in action.

This hexagram combines five yangs and one yin in the trigrams *Tui* and *Ch'ien*, marsh and Heaven. The five yangs are bound together ready to sweep away the weak yin line. The power of corrupt men is on the wane and is being replaced by wise leadership. The move towards re-establishing harmony and cooperation must begin locally and without force. An honest and virtuous personality is the best weapon for weakening corrupt authority. Since the marsh is on top of the mountain in the *Kuai* hexagram we can expect a rainstorm which will provide moisture for everything on earth. A selfish man warily guards his wealth, but a generous man bestows his knowledge on everyone he meets.

Line of Change

FIRST NINE

He steps out boldly. He sets forth, but not to victory. He will regret this.

This line is compared to someone who is young and energetic but also inexperienced. You may be capable, but if you try to deal with too much too quickly you will inevitably meet difficulties. Before you do anything, find out exactly how capable you are and give some thought to the difficulties ahead.

SECOND NINE

He stands almost ready whilst others arm in the night. There is nothing to fear.

Nobody will challenge you if you are cautious, modest and reasonable. You have nothing to fear.

THIRD NINE

He puts his best face forward and this brings misfortune. The wise man is securely positioned. He walks above and encounters rain, and is therefore soaked and annoyed. There is no cause for regret.

Try not to be too hasty. If you are in a delicate situation, be careful. Do not anger the people you want to be rid of, but at the same time do not raise suspicions amongst the people you want as friends. The young may seem tough. Do not worry. Carry on doing what you know is right.

FOURTH NINE

The skin on his buttocks has been stripped away and he walks with difficulty. If he were led like a sheep there would be no worries. However, if he were to hear what is said he would not believe it.

Beware of being obstinate like this fourth line. To insist on doing things your own way, regardless of circumstances, only invites disaster. Because you do not understand situations very well you tend to misinterpret good advice.

FIFTH NINE

When he sorts out weeds he is secure in his determined attitude. There will be no mistake in following the correct path.

This line is the leader of the other four yang lines. Avoid being like these yang lines which are easily won over by the yin line's superficially sweet words. Your actions should be resolute. Be true to what you know is right.

TOP SIX

He does not stand prepared. This will eventually bring evil.

Bad times are slipping away. The honest will soon replace the corrupt. Follow the advice of the holy man who said it is never too late to admit your faults and correct your ways.

KOU

To Meet

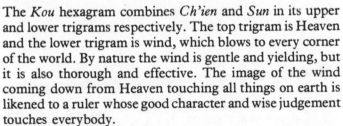

To meet. The woman is strong and tough. Do not get married to a woman like this.

The *Kou* hexagram combines *Ch'ien* and *Sun* in its upper and lower trigrams respectively. The top trigram is Heaven and the lower trigram is wind, which blows to every corner of the world. By nature the wind is gentle and yielding, but it is also thorough and effective. The image of the wind coming down from Heaven touching all things on earth is likened to a ruler whose good character and wise judgement touches everybody.

The five yin and one yang lines represent one woman and five men. Because the woman seems delicate and harmless the men unsuspectingly allow her into their company. Because she is always in men's company she is determined to win power, and her arrogance makes her totally unsuitable for power. Certain things are predestined to meet but others are totally unsuited to do so.

Line of Change

FIRST SIX

He should be restrained with an iron brake. Proper behaviour will bring good fortune. If he goes forward in any way he will encounter misfortune. He is like a thin pig who rushes around.

Your emotions should always be kept under control, like a car's brakes. This line is like a young woman who has left home for the first time. Although five men have fallen in love with her she modestly chooses one man for a husband. You too must not be overwhelmed by flattery and attention. You will be fortunate.

SECOND NINE

There is nothing wrong in the fact that he has a packet of fish. Do not give this to guests.

Two people can work happily together in a marriage. You cannot expect a successful relationship if a third person tries to join in.

THIRD NINE

The skin on his buttocks has been stripped away and he has difficulty walking. There is danger but he does not make any major mistakes.

At the moment your movements are severely limited, as though you have an injured hip. Your circumstances, however, prevent you from falling into bad company or entering into a disastrous business partnership.

FOURTH NINE

He has a packet but no fish. There will be misfortune.

Due to a chance meeting with the Second Nine, the First Six has abandoned this line. Do not behave like the First Six. Do not leave people because you think they are unimportant. One day you may turn to them for help and they will no longer be there.

FIFTH NINE

The melon is covered by the tree's leaves. Part of it is hidden. It comes as though from Heaven.

When a willow leaf is wrapped around a slice of melon, not only is the melon preserved but the bitter and sweet flavours also flow into one another. If you lead others, be prepared to take responsibility, but do not overexert your authority. Appoint your colleagues carefully. Listen to others. Look for men who are honest and courageous.

TOP NINE

He meets others with his horns. This will bring regret. There will be no mistakes.

This obstinate line is as tough as an animal's horn. If two arrogant and obstinate people clash they cannot expect harmony. As long as you are true to your character there is no need to worry.

TS'UI

To Collect

HEXAGRAM 45

To collect. Success. The king approaches the temple. It is good to see the great man. There will be success. It is good to behave properly. The use of large offerings brings good fortune. To move forward in any direction will also bring good fortune.

The *Ts'ui* hexagram combines the marsh and earth in its upper and lower trigrams, *Tui* and *K'un*. The trigrams are naturally compromising and cheerful. The Fifth Nine is virtuous and obstinate and will work happily with the yielding and virtuous Second Six. The water flowing over the earth collects in lakes and marshes and nourishes the land. It is a good time to join others and work for a common cause.

Line of Change

FIRST SIX

He is sincere in his wish, but if he does not carry it out there may sometimes be confusion, sometimes a coming together. He calls out. Then his tears give way to smiles. He does not mind. He goes forward and there will be no mistakes.

Although you are more and more successful in your work, others may try to disrupt your plans. You should turn to someone who is experienced for guidance just as the First Six turns to the Fourth Nine for help.

SECOND SIX

He is led forward and there is great fortune. There are no mistakes. As long as he is sincere even the smallest offering will bring advantages.

45 TS'UI

This is a time of growth. At the moment you have fresh energy, but be careful. It is easy to misuse newfound power. Be sincere and honest. You will be lucky.

THIRD SIX

He tries to bring unity, but then he sighs. He can find no advantages anywhere. There will be no mistakes if he goes forward, but there may be slight cause for regret.

At times you try very hard to make progress but are still left feeling dissatisfied. Since this line is helped by *K'un*'s wisdom, you too must share responsibility for projects. Share your worries with someone else.

FOURTH NINE

Great fortune. There will be no mistakes.

When intelligent men meet together they cannot fail to influence the people who come in contact with them. If you are part of a committed group you can work effectively for a common cause. Wisdom is like marsh water which moistens the earth. In turn the earth nourishes plants, animals and people.

FIFTH NINE

He uses his dignified position to unite them together. This is no mistake. If someone is insincere, then admirable, persistent and good behaviour will ensure that distress disappears.

Like an emperor you must choose colleagues on merit. Select workers who are competent and honest, men who stand out from the crowd.

TOP SIX

He sighs and weeps floods of tears. There will be no mistakes.

Do not expect continued success. One day you may be rich and popular, the next poor and without friends. Try to understand that this is the way life goes.

SHENG

Rising Up

HEXAGRAM 46

Rising up. There will be great success. He tries to see the great man. He does not worry. Moving to the south will bring good fortune.

Sung combines *K'un* and *Sun*, earth and wind, in its upper and lower trigrams. When seeds are planted in the earth they grow up through the soil to flower in the light. This is used to describe a period of promotion and prosperity. After the assembly of the previous hexagram the country and the people become stronger. Everything is rapidly growing and expanding and will eventually reach its limit. Inevitably this prosperity will attract untrustworthy characters who can spot an opportunity to exploit this boom.

Normally a leader who has a yielding character will appreciate the difficulty of employing staff who have obstinate manners. However, if the staff are obedient they will soon be promoted. Promotion alleviates worry and enables a man to expand his business, particularly in the south, which is *Li*, a bright area. He now has a more compromising manner, works happily with his boss and will therefore be fortunate.

A wise man is willing to listen and work alongside others, he gradually saves his money and eventually becomes wealthy. His character develops in the same way, so that his heart is bright and understanding.

Line of Change

FIRST SIX

He rises up and is welcomed. There will be extremely good fortune.

153

Like this line you should be willing to give way and accept others. Learn to work happily alongside your boss and soon you will be promoted.

SECOND NINE

If he is sincere then even the smallest offerings will be advantageous. There will be no mistakes.

If you are in charge of staff, treat them well and in return they will be keen to work for you. If your staff respect and trust you they do not need to flatter you.

THIRD NINE

He goes up into an empty town.

This line is at the top of the lower trigram now, but if it should step forward it would find itself at the bottom of the *K'un* trigram. Likewise you may be promoted, but in name only, not in terms of real authority.

FOURTH SIX

The king uses him to make offerings for success on Mount Ch'i. There will be good fortune. There will be no mistakes.

This is the Prime Minister's line. Whatever his merits, like you he cannot be promoted because the next line is filled by a more powerful person (the Emperor).

FIFTH SIX

He behaves properly and is fortunate. He mounts the steps.

Make a point of promoting trustworthy and hard-working staff. You will be rewarded by their hard work.

TOP SIX

He rises up from the dark. It is helpful to be unceasingly persistent.

You have been through a time of rapid promotion, but it has now reached its limit. Do not expect continual good fortune. Do not be like a man who is so bewitched by the idea of profit that he never makes any real profit. The holy man cautions against avarice.

K'UN

To Surround and Wear Out

HEXAGRAM 47

*To surround and wear out. There will be success. Keep going.
The great man has good fortune. There will be no mistakes. He
has a speech to make but he is not believed.*

The *K'un* hexagram combines *K'an* and *Tui*, water and
marsh, in its lower and upper trigrams. The marsh
eventually becomes dry as the water seeps downwards; in
the same way a nation or a family which overspends runs
into distressing economic problems. The problem, however, can be resolved, depending on his *Tao* – his reason and
his understanding character. The holy man said that
someone who is suffering must search his heart to find the
right way, and as long as he is capable and virtuous he will
find the path out of his distress.

The First Six, the Third Six and the Top Six are all
surrounded by yin and cannot be clearly seen. A marsh
usually holds water unless it is particularly porous; a
country also remains relatively stable unless it has corrupt
leaders. The citizens of the country will naturally suffer,
but they must use this distress to harden their resolve.

Line of Change

FIRST SIX

*He is sitting exhausted under the barren trees. He wanders into
a dreary valley. Nothing happens for three years.*

If you lack particular skills or intelligence you will go
unnoticed like the twisted roots of a tree hidden below the
soil. When you are struggling to improve yourself very few
people will offer support.

SECOND NINE

He is sitting exhausted amid his wine and meat. The person with the red knee bands is coming. It is helpful to offer sacrifices. Moving forward brings bad fortune, but there will be no mistakes.

Everybody is fond of eating and drinking, but do not make yourself ill from excess. In the right company and right place it is fine to be drunk. At other times you will make a fool of yourself.

THIRD SIX

He is sitting exhausted among the stones. He grasps at thorns. He goes into his palace and does not see his wife. There will be bad fortune.

This is a time of loss. Although this line is on the top of the lower trigram it cannot look to the top six for help. You are going through a difficult time.

FOURTH NINE

He proceeds very slowly. He is sitting exhausted by his golden carriage. There is good reason for his sadness but all will be well in the end.

There is a clash of natures between the Fourth and Fifth Nines. Because you are stubborn but honest your actions may have hurt others. Your way is temporarily blocked. At the moment people slander you. Be patient and you will pull through.

FIFTH NINE

His nose and feet are cut off. He is sitting, exhausted by the person with the scarlet knee bands. Everything is slow but well. It is helpful to make sacrifices.

This line cannot be helped by the Second Nine. It is being punished, just as in old China a person's nose and foot were cut off for an offence. This is used to describe the Emperor's suffering. He governs alone due to lack of care from his officials. Like the Emperor, you may have enough influence to deal with a crisis, but do not expect immediate results. A system is not easily changed. Be determined and patient. Put your reforms into effect cautiously.

He is sitting exhausted among the creeping plants. He moves in a certain way and says, 'If I move I shall be sorry.' If he is able to be sorry and then moves forward there will be good fortune.

You are trapped by complications and cannot see an escape route. If you move forward you will ensnare yourself more deeply; if you stay put you will never recover. Your position is reflected in this line. It is in more distress than any other line in the hexagram. You will have difficulty making quick decisions if you are confused. Do not rely too heavily on others or become too involved. Act wisely and all will be well.

CHING

The Well

HEXAGRAM 48

The well. The town may be moved, but the well may not. It does not shrink or grow. People come and go to draw water from the well. If they cannot quite reach the water with a rope or if the bucket breaks, there will be bad fortune.

Ching represents a well dug into the ground. The upper trigram *K'an*, water, is shaped like a well and *Sun*, wind, is compromising and follows the source of the water under the ground. These are the two most important factors for siting a well, a flowing and adaptable source of water.

Water is an essential resource for everybody; cities and countries may change but a well can stand for ever. When you attempt to draw water you must carefully lower the bucket down the middle of the well otherwise the bucket will be shattered on the wall of the well. The well therefore cannot fulfil its function unless you use it carefully. The well supplies an endless source of water but does not ask for anything in return, just as a wise man gives unconditional support and advice, thus enriching the lives of those who listen to him.

Line of Change

FIRST SIX

He does not drink from the muddy well. No creatures come to an old well.

If well water is dirty you would naturally look for a fresh supply; likewise if your government is corrupt you will look elsewhere for leaders. The holy man said, 'Harsh government is worse than a tiger.'

The well has sprung a leak and the fish and water spurt forth.
The broken jug leaks.

If you have a responsible job, make sure you have a good general understanding of your subject. Nobody will support you if you continually make mistakes.

THIRD NINE

Although the well has been cleaned no one uses it. This is a weight upon the heart because it can be used. If the king was clever he and others could benefit from this.

If your well water was once muddy but is now clear you will still hesitate before drinking it. If you are wrongly accused, however much you proclaim your innocence you will still be guilty in the public eye. It takes a good deal of courage and patience to clear your name and re-establish your reputation.

FOURTH SIX

The well is well lined. There will be no mistakes.

You feel trapped. There is little room for manoeuvre. There is little you can do. Behave normally. Try not to upset others.

FIFTH NINE

The well has clear, cold water which can be drunk.

A good and honest character is as clean and cool as spring water. Just as spring water is never murky, so your judgement should never dim. You will be well respected if you are not easily flattered or influenced.

TOP SIX

He draws from the well without difficulty because it is open. He is sincere. This will bring great good fortune.

The well is brimming with fresh water, likewise your country is content with its government. A good leader's strength lies in his careful judgements and actions. Your life is shaped by his wise decisions.

KO

Change

Change. He is believed in his own right time. There will be great success. It is helpful to behave properly. Any cause for regret disappears.

Ko means an animal's pelt and combines *Li* and *Tui* in its lower and upper trigrams. Since *Li* is fire and *Tui* is marsh they will easily destroy each other unless they are used wisely; for example, fire can be used to boil the water which will peel away an animal's pelt. On the other hand water can extinguish fire, just as two girls married to the same man cannot expect a harmonious relationship. Their relationship may improve if they change the situation, but success will depend on what has to be altered and the time chosen. Conditions for change must be right so that the old can be destroyed and the new can be built.

The fiery rays of the sun shine down harmoniously on the marsh water at different levels according to the time of day and the season. A wise man always notices the seasons and keeps check on the alterations of the natural world as well as Heaven's way.

Line of Change

FIRST NINE

He is bound in the skin of a yellow cow.

If you are on the bottom rung of the promotion ladder you are unlikely to win the admiration of the management. Work hard. You have done your best if you are able to sail through the rough patches.

SECOND SIX

When his time comes he is able to make changes. Initiating action will bring extremely good fortune. There will be no mistakes.

If you have the expertise and confidence of a civil official you can carry out any operation smoothly.

THIRD NINE

Initiating action will bring bad fortune. Even if he behaves properly there is danger. If he wishes to change things he will need to discuss them three times, and then people will have confidence in him.

This line gets no help from the First Nine or the Second Six. You too will not be offered any help if you rush headlong into changes and new plans.

FOURTH NINE

The need to repent disappears. He is believed. He alters the way things are and is fortunate.

When things are in disarray rely on a strong yang character rather than a malleable yin character. You will obviously have confidence in and respect for a determined and courageous man.

FIFTH NINE

The great man changes like a tiger. Even though he has not yet consulted the oracle people have confidence in him.

A good leader's character and abilities are strong and awe-inspiring like the pattern on a tiger's skin. There is no need to consult the oracle about his future. You can trust him. Whatever plans he has will be carried through successfully.

TOP SIX

The wise man changes like a leopard, whereas the lesser man simply recomposes his face. To advance will bring bad fortune. To continue behaving correctly will bring good fortune.

Like this line, you are resolute enough to be successful yet tolerant enough to care for others. The best leader ensures that everyone benefits from a revolution and not just the select few. Do not, however, expect an immediate reward for your actions.

TING

The Cooking Pot

Ting, *the three-legged cooking pot. Great fortune and success.*

The *Ting* hexagram combines *Sun* and *Li*, wind and fire, in its lower and upper trigrams. *Ting*'s function is fulfilled when food is boiled by fire in order to produce a meal. Once the meal is prepared the Emperor invites many well-known people to a banquet, and he in turn benefits from their wisdom. Just as food is boiled gradually, you have to work step by step towards promotion. The food is cooked quickly with the help of the determined Second Nine, and likewise an organization will be successful if they have a dependable workforce.

Line of Change

FIRST SIX

The cooking pot is upturned and its feet are in the air. This is helpful for getting rid of useless stuff. A concubine is useful because of the son she has. There will be no mistakes.

If one leg of a cooking pot is shorter than the others it will easily fall over. But every now and then the pot has to be refilled and the residue cleared away. In the same way you should get rid of any bad habits before setting out on a new venture.

SECOND NINE

The cooking pot has food inside it. My colleagues are jealous but they cannot harm me. There will be good fortune.

Do not leave yourself open to criticism. Be able and careful in your work.

THIRD NINE

The handles on the cooking pot have been changed. He is halted in his progress. The pheasant's juicy meat is not eaten. The rain comes and sadness ends. In the end there will be good fortune.

If you cook a pheasant in a pot without handles you will not be able to pull the meat out. The pheasant may rot but at least you will know how to cook it next time. Many worthwhile opportunities may slip by you. Learn from your mistakes. Use your experience to make the most of new opportunities.

FOURTH NINE

The legs of the cooking pot are broken. The noble's food is spilt and his clothes are soiled. There will be bad fortune.

Do not put a weak person in a responsible position. You would lose confidence in a cook if he were to break the cooking pot's legs, overturn it and spill your food on the floor. Everyone suffers if an incompetent man is given an important post.

FIFTH SIX

The cooking pot has yellow ears and gold handles. It is helpful to continue behaving properly.

The cooking pot is in perfect shape and you can make good use of it. This is a good time. The Second and Fourth Nines are like the pot's handles and are supporting the Fifth Six. Never underestimate the value of a good leader. He is like gold – pure, honest and unprejudiced.

TOP NINE

The cooking pot has rings of jade. There will be very good fortune. Everything here works to his advantage.

This line, which is influential, can be compared to the rod used to lift the red-hot pot off the fire. Like the rod, you have an important job to do. You must be as pure as pure jade.

CHEN

Shock

Shock. Success. The shock comes but he looks out and is seen with cheerful words on his lips. Although the shock terrifies everyone for a hundred miles around, he does not drop the sacrificial spoon and cup.

The lower and upper trigrams of *Chen* are identical, both are *Chen*, thunder and movement. This hexagram is exceedingly determined and strong, particularly the First and Fourth Nines.

The power of thunder is immense as it rolls across the sky with sufficient strength to kill people or animals. There is nothing to compare with its power. The first yang line stands below the two yin lines and has the power to shudder violently. Legends say that all the Chinese emperors came from *Chen* so that Heaven and earth are moved by their power.

Chen's way is worthy and good and nothing can stand in its way. People have to alter and change, and you can learn to respect but not be fearful of a sudden and close clap of thunder. If you have a character like *Chen* in your position of authority, you will protect others.

Line of Change

FIRST NINE

The shock comes and he looks around carefully, but then cheerful words come to his lips. There will be good fortune.

Once you have survived a frightening time you will know how to deal with fear in future. This line is perplexed because it is the first line to hear the roll of thunder and it does not know how to respond.

He is in danger when the shock comes. He loses his treasures. He climbs nine hills. He does not go in search of his treasures but finds them again after seven days.

On hearing the thunder this line has sped to safety leaving the money behind. Do not worry too much over loss. Sometimes it is inevitable. Whatever it is that you have lost will return in time.

THIRD SIX

The shock makes him very upset and disturbed. The shock makes him act but there is nothing wrong in this.

Something disastrous is about to happen. Like the Third Six, you must face it alone. The catastrophe you fear will only frighten you. It will not cause any real harm.

FOURTH NINE

The shock makes him as sluggish as mud.

If you are weak and timid you will collapse in the face of danger. Be careful. Do not let others see you totally confused.

FIFTH SIX

He comes and goes and the shock threatens danger. However, there is no problem because he has things to do.

The *Chen* hexagram is now in an extremely dangerous position but it has the strength to resist threats. Warn others when problems appear. Ensure your own safety by taking sufficient precautions.

TOP SIX

The shock causes him to be dismayed and he looks around anxiously. Initiating action will bring bad fortune. He will have acted rightly if he moves before the shock reaches him although it has reached his neighbourhood. His family, however, may grumble about him.

On hearing a sudden clap of thunder you may be safe, but you know that someone, somewhere, has been hurt. Once you have seen others suffer you will learn not to make the same mistake yourself.

KEN

Resting

Resting. Resting his back, he is not able to feel his body. He goes into the courtyard. He does not see his own people. There will be no mistakes.

The *Ken* hexagram combines *Ken* in its upper and lower trigrams. *Ken* is like an unmovable mountain which supports running spring water and flowering trees on its slopes. In the same way the human back does not show any feelings but it supports the whole body.

Whatever shape mountains may be, and whatever lies on their slopes, their characters are the same. A wise man is like a mountain; he may be surrounded by many distractions, but he is not affected by the world around him.

You should behave according to how you feel and not what others dictate. If plans have to be carried out, work them through; if it is time to rest, then give yourself time to relax.

Line of Change

FIRST SIX

There is nothing wrong with resting his toes. It is helpful for him always to behave in a true manner.

When you start a job, do as much as you can. You will soon be promoted. The holy man advises you to build solid foundations so that your success will last for ever.

SECOND SIX

He rests his legs. He is unable to save the person whom he follows and is uneasy in his heart.

Your job may not carry much responsibility but your effort

---

is essential for the smooth running of your company. Basic administration has an important role, like your legs. They control your body and dictate whether you move forward or stand still.

THIRD NINE

He rests his loins. He puts his ribs aside from him. There is danger and his heart burns with anxious excitement.

If your back is broken your body is paralysed. Likewise your mistakes hinder cooperation with everyone else.

FOURTH SIX

He rests his body. There will be no mistakes.

Be like this line, which is gentle and honest. Consider how you feel and how you should react before doing or saying anything.

FIFTH SIX

He rests his jaw. His speech is composed. Any cause for regret disappears.

When you have a near escape, control your reactions. Do not let your face give away your true feelings.

TOP NINE

He remains resting with devotion. There will be good fortune.

This line has reached the mountain's peak and can go no further. Everything has its limit. Do not try to overdo it.

CHIEN
Gradual Development

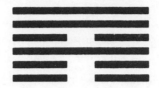

Gradual development. The woman is married. There will be good fortune. It is helpful to behave properly.

The *Chien* hexagram combines *Ken* and *Sun* in its lower and upper trigrams. *Ken* is the mountain and *Sun* is wind. Trees which flourish on a mountain side must be given time to put down roots so they can withstand heavy rains and powerful winds. We must also grow through experience and understanding, otherwise we will easily stumble, like a young sapling which is uprooted by a storm.

When a father hands his business over to his son, the son cannot be expected to deal completely with every crisis, just as a young couple must first of all understand each other before they commit themselves to marriage.

You cannot work independently of others or hope to be famous within a short time. Progress is gradual and the process of learning is endless, so all your thoughts and actions should fit in accordingly with the pace of events around you. A wise man lives in accordance with *Chien*: he attains to honesty and virtue, and when he achieves this he uses his wisdom to guide others.

Line of Change

FIRST SIX

The geese gradually draw near to the shore. The younger son is in danger. Although he is talked about there will be no mistakes.

You must be like a young goose who follows his parents' example. Geese always circle above their landing area to check for dangers beforehand, and so the young goose avoids being trapped. Respect the experience of your elders. Take life step by step.

SECOND SIX

The geese gradually draw near to the cliff, and here they eat and drink happily and contentedly. There will be good fortune.

Do not be greedy. Geese know that the hunter uses rock salt to attract them. However hungry they might be, they are always cautious before coming in to land. You too must be patient and careful. Do not take unnecessary risks.

THIRD NINE

The geese gradually draw near to the plains. This is like a husband who goes out but does not return, or like a wife who is pregnant but who does not have the baby. There will be bad fortune. It is good to fight off thieves.

Do your work quickly and carefully. Do not rush headlong into new ventures. Give a thought to others so that you do not jeopardize their lives.

FOURTH SIX

The geese gradually draw near to the tree and land on its flat branches. There will be no mistakes.

If you take on many responsibilities you must also expect to face many difficulties. It is important that you are in tune with your environment, then you will find a safe way to carry out your duties.

FIFTH NINE

The geese gradually draw near the mountain. This is like a wife who does not become pregnant for three years. In the end she conceives as nothing can prevent this. There will be good fortune.

Although you are capable, it is easy to be misled. Cooperation with others is essential because we are all working for a common goal.

53 CHIEN

The geese gradually draw near to the highest heights. Their feathers can be used for the ritual dance. There will be good fortune.

Work on your career step by step, and you will soon find yourself at the top of the ladder. Like the wild geese, approach your work cautiously. To avoid confusion deal with problems in the order in which they arrive. Once you are experienced the trivial aspects of life will not worry you.

KUEI MEI

Marrying the Younger Sister

HEXAGRAM 54

Marrying the younger sister. Initiating actions will bring bad fortune. There are no advantages here.

This hexagram combines *Tui* and *Chen*, marsh and thunder, in its lower and upper trigrams. *Kuei* is a woman of marriageable age and *Mei* is a young woman. In ancient China a woman acted as a go-between for two interested parties, and the couple could be married once the man had asked the girl's permission. Man's nature is as strong as thunder, although he can sometimes be very moody, and a woman's nature is weak and gentle as water. Once the thunder and lightning have subsided, clouds turn to rain which falls on the marsh.

The Second Nine and the Fifth Six are yang inside and yin outside, which are not the right positions. The hexagram's text indicates a happy marriage as long as the woman follows in the man's footsteps, but if she tries to be more dominant then the marriage cannot last. A wise man advises people to commit themselves to marriage for life, but if they make a mistake at the beginning they will always regret it.

Line of Change

FIRST NINE

The younger sister is married as a subordinate to the first wife. This is like a lame man who manages to get along. To advance will bring good fortune.

If you are young, healthy and dependable, prove your worth to others. Fight for opportunities and you will be successful.

SECOND NINE

The one-eyed person is able to see. It is helpful for a man to

behave in the same way as a recluse does.

This line is imperfect, like a woman who has lost an eye. Her husband no longer loves her, but she is still his wife and remains devoted to him. Like the wife, you must not give up hope. Be loyal regardless of circumstances.

THIRD SIX

The younger sister is ready to be married but she is in a lowly position. When she returns she is married off as a concubine.

You have unfortunately taken up a position below your usual standards. You want too much too quickly. You are like a younger sister who, seeing her older sister happily married, decides to be her brother-in-law's concubine. This behaviour is thoughtless and totally unsuitable for a woman.

FOURTH NINE

The younger sister spins out the time to her marriage, but she will eventually be married.

There is nothing wrong in postponing a plan as long as you have a good reason for doing so. If a girl does not wish to marry the same man as her sister she has every right to postpone the wedding until she can marry legally.

FIFTH SIX

Emperor I gave his younger sister in marriage but her embroidered clothes were not as gorgeous as those of her attendants. The moon is almost full. There will be good fortune.

A good woman is far more interested in a man's character than in his money or looks. The Chinese say that you will be fortunate if you are as honourable and pure as the full moon.

TOP SIX

The woman carries a basket but it does not contain any food. The gentleman stabs the sheep but no blood comes out. There is nothing to be gained here.

This line is at the weakest point. Never act under false pretences. A man and woman who pretend to be in love with each other will have a disastrous marriage. You will not gain anything by deceiving others.

FENG

Prosperity

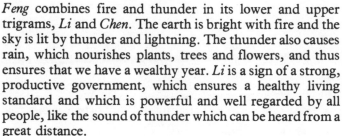

Prosperity. Success. There is nothing to worry about because the king achieves everything. He should be like the sun at midday.

Feng combines fire and thunder in its lower and upper trigrams, *Li* and *Chen*. The earth is bright with fire and the sky is lit by thunder and lightning. The thunder also causes rain, which nourishes plants, trees and flowers, and thus ensures that we have a wealthy year. *Li* is a sign of a strong, productive government, which ensures a healthy living standard and which is powerful and well regarded by all people, like the sound of thunder which can be heard from a great distance.

Because the ground is covered in light and the thunder rules strongly in the sky there is a wealthy, strong situation which could possibly collapse or be destroyed by others. Because *Li* is so bright there is no need to worry, there are no dark or unintelligible forces around. When the thunder and lightning disappear darkness will come, just as the full moon eventually wanes or the noon sun begins to sink. One moment Heaven and earth may be vigorous and abundant, and the next they may be dull and sparse, because the world continues to grow and diminish according to the seasons. This is how our lives and spirits are also guided. A wise man must be strong like the lightning, determining the path between right and wrong and justly apportioning punishment.

Line of Change

FIRST NINE

He meets his supreme ruler. There is nothing wrong in the fact

Because you have a good relationship with your boss, do not presume that you can be rude to him.

SECOND SIX

His prosperity is like a curtain. At midday he can see the stars in the Dipper constellation. When he goes out he is treated with suspicion and hatred. There will be fortune if he is encouraged to follow confidently.

You will be viewed with suspicion if you hide your real intentions from others. Do not attempt too much in uncertain times. Although this line is bright, when it attempts to work with the Fifth Six it is obscured by thunder and dark clouds. Be sincere and open. Everything will eventually work out well.

THIRD NINE

His prosperity is like a banner through which he can see the smallest stars at midday. He breaks his right arm but there will be no mistakes.

This line is surrounded by walls so large and thick that it can hardly see. Do not attempt any important projects if you do not completely understand what you are doing.

FOURTH NINE

His prosperity is like a curtain, through which he can see the stars in the Dipper constellation at midday. He meets his king and they are alike. There will be good fortune.

If your self-esteem is too great you will blind yourself to the real issues. Someone must rescue you from this darkness so you can see clearly again.

FIFTH SIX

The various parts come together. He is praised and congratulated. There will be good fortune.

You may not be wealthy or strong, but if you work with reliable and honest company you have no need to worry. Although this line is weak it is strengthened by the Fourth Nine and protected by the Second Six.

His own household is prosperous. He encloses his family inside and peers out through the gate, but does not see anyone there. He does not see anything for three years. There will be misfortune.

Do not abuse your wealth by showing off or over-indulgence. Be careful and your money will last for ever.

LÜ

The Traveller

HEXAGRAM 56

The traveller. Minor success. If the traveller behaves properly there will be good fortune.

The *Lü* hexagram is the opposite of *Feng*, both in its order and meaning, and it combines *Ken* and *Li* in its lower and upper trigrams. *Ken* is mountain and *Li* is fire. *Lü* means to move away, to travel or to emigrate. There comes a time when you have to move out of the shelter of the home into a new environment, and once your vision is broadened you learn to adapt and use the environment. If you are travelling and learning you must be careful and adaptable, not obstinate. *Ken*, which is inside the *Lü* hexagram, is quiet and even-tempered, and *Li*, which is on the outside, is intelligent and understanding. You must have a quiet and understanding heart to realize what is happening around you and follow the rules.

The mountain is bright with fire, and a wise man lives in accordance with this fiery mountain by exerting his wisdom, exercising caution in the use of punishment and stepping in to stop quarrels and litigation.

Line of Change

FIRST SIX

Because the traveller is engaged in worthless activities he brings disaster upon himself.

Always act sensibly and honestly in a strange town. Never become greedy. If you do land in trouble nobody will help you.

SECOND SIX

The traveller arrives at an inn, carrying his goods. He obtains the services of a dependable and upright servant.

If you decide to leave your home and family, make sure you travel with sufficient funds and a trustworthy friend.

THIRD NINE

The traveller burns down the inn. He loses his faithful servant. Even if he behaves properly there is danger.

Do not be argumentative amongst strangers. If you are travelling with a friend you need his companionship, so treat him well. Travelling is difficult enough without making problems for yourself.

FOURTH NINE

The traveller is in a shelter and has his goods and an ox with him. 'My heart is not at ease.'

When you are travelling you may not be offered the job you want. You have to accept the work and hospitality you are given.

FIFTH SIX

He shoots at a pheasant but loses his arrow. Eventually he is praised and given an official post.

Make sure that you understand the protocol of a foreign country. Although an emperor's envoy shoots at a pheasant on his journey he does not immediately kill it but loses his arrow. The emperor hears of the envoy's action and gives him appropriate honours. You too will be welcomed by strangers if you act appropriately.

TOP NINE

He is like a bird which burns its own nest. Initially the traveller laughs, but then he weeps. Because of the changes he loses his ox. There will be bad fortune.

Do not revel in another man's misfortune. Nobody will have any sympathy for you when you have problems of your own. If you refuse to apologize you are like an ox which charges through the fence into another farm and can never return.

SUN

Gentle and Yielding

Gentle and yielding. Minor success. It is helpful to advance. It is also helpful to see the great man.

Two *Sun* trigrams are combined together in this hexagram, which is the wind blowing into every corner. The yin line is at the lowest point below two yang lines, which is an indication of obedience and willingness. Because the wind is mobile it cannot aspire to lofty aims but takes a middle position, like a young officer who is praised by his seniors because of his obedience and respect. *Sun* is very weak and follows orders from above; therefore if it has a bad leader its progress is seriously hindered. A wise man's decisions are like the wind: once he has given an order everyone will obey his command.

Line of Change

FIRST SIX

He advances and retreats. It is helpful to be well prepared and to behave like a soldier.

Do not be weak and indecisive, like the wind in the trees. However, if you are starting a new job your indecisiveness will be overlooked as long as you are obedient.

SECOND NINE

He sits quietly under the bed. He uses diviners and magicians, causing great confusion. There will be good fortune and no mistakes.

This line causes trouble because it refuses to bow down to the Fifth Nine. Obey orders. Willing and obedient workers ensure a successful business.

THIRD NINE

He is persistent but gentle. This is regrettable.

While it is advisable to be obedient and thoughtful, you must also consider your own opinions. You will be sorry if you mindlessly follow the wrong advice.

FOURTH SIX

There are no regrets. He catches three kinds of creatures in the field.

Use your weaknesses to your own advantage. You are in a good position to help others.

FIFTH NINE

Proper behaviour brings good fortune. There is nothing to regret. Everything he does is advantageous. The start may not be good but everything will work out well in the end. There will be three days before the changes occur. Allow three days after the changes. There will be good fortune.

You have the strength to encourage and help others. Before doing anything, think carefully. You will succeed if you correct your faults at the very beginning.

TOP NINE

He sits quietly under the bed. He loses his goods and his ox. However well he behaves there will be misfortune.

You are like this line, determined but easily influenced. Even though you are on good terms with everyone you may be used or insulted.

TUI

Happiness

HEXAGRAM 58

Happiness. Success. It is advantageous to behave properly and firmly.

The upper and lower trigrams are both *Tui* and they represent happiness and willingness to accept what is happening. People will respond to the kindness they feel from others. Because *Tui* is a marsh it provides moisture for all plants and animals, which are grateful because they are cared for. Kindness is endless because it follows Heaven's reason and suits everyone.

A wise man is like the life-giving marsh water because he treats everyone equally as friends.

Line of Change

FIRST NINE

Happiness and harmony. There will be good fortune.

A cheerful outlook is a good way to start a career. Be willing and open. You will never come under suspicion.

SECOND NINE

Confidence and happiness. There will be good fortune. Every sadness disappears.

Be trustworthy, cheerful and determined. You will be fortunate. Do not waste your time on trivial pastimes.

THIRD SIX

Happiness is coming. There will be misfortune.

Do not pretend to feel emotion just to please others. Smile

because you feel happy. You do not need to pursue happiness, it comes from within.

FOURTH NINE

He deliberates about what will make him happy but this does not satisfy him. The things he is involved with are diseased but he will be happy.

You are unsettled. Some things please you, other things worry you. Divide your worries and pleasures into two groups as though you are cutting a stone in two. Do this and you will be lucky.

FIFTH NINE

He is confident despite the disasters around him. This is dangerous.

The holy man cautions against too much trust in others. Someone will betray your unquestioning trust.

TOP SIX

Seductive happiness.

Do not waste your time trying to please others. You are so busy flattering others that you will lose your own identity.

HUAN

Scattered

Scattered. Success. The king travels to his temple. It is helpful to cross the great river. It is also good to behave properly.

The *Huan* hexagram combines *K'an* and *Sun*, water and wind, in its lower and upper trigrams. The hexagram indicates departure, but there will be an effort to gather again so that everything can take its natural way through. When wind blows across the surface of a lake it causes ripples, and when the events around you are unsteady you will naturally be troubled. Even when things are running smoothly you can cause complications by corrupt scheming.

In the past Chinese emperors have united the people by building temples to their predecessors where sacrifices can be offered to Heaven. The citizens are encouraged to remember the virtues of past emperors so that everyone can work with the same mind and heart.

Line of Change

FIRST SIX

He rescues with the strength of a horse. There will be good fortune.

You will have difficulty concentrating on a new project. However, before long you will establish a routine.

SECOND NINE

When everything is scattered abroad he hurries to a place of safety. There is nothing to be anxious about.

You are trying to concentrate on an important matter. First of all get yourself organized, then organize others.

He disregards his own person. This is no cause for regret.

Something unlucky is about to happen because of danger on the water trigram. Change your surroundings. Develop your career elsewhere.

FOURTH SIX

He breaks up his group. There will be great fortune. He scatters and then gathers in a mound; ordinary people would never have considered doing this.

Your bad luck is passing. A good period is on the way. Good friends have always stuck by you, but now you meet new friends. You will be as fortunate as gold which glistens after treatment by fire.

FIFTH NINE

He is dripping with sweat when he loudly cries out. He has done nothing wrong. He scatters the king's offices. There is nothing wrong in this.

If you are a good leader you have the determination and strength to wipe out corruption. You must inspire others. There is no need to worry, you will not make any mistakes.

TOP NINE

He scatters his blood. He departs. He leaves and then keeps his distance. There will be no mistakes.

There is no point in staying in a bad situation. In ancient China a stone needle was used to drain dirty blood. Use your energy to get rid of old habits. Inject new blood into your life.

CHIEH

Limitations

Limitations. Success. If the limitations are too strict they should not be allowed to go on for too long.

The *Tui* and *K'an* trigrams are combined in the hexagram *Chieh*, which means to control. *Tui* is marsh and *K'an* is water. Although water is one of the essential natural resources it can cause disaster if it is not carefully controlled. The marsh requires a certain amount of water to maintain the life of plants and animals; too much water causes flooding and too little causes drought. This hexagram advises a controlled and adequate way of life. *Chieh* must be a central point which should not be overused or underused, as this would only affect your life and the lives of others. You should not be too harsh on yourself; do not be miserly or overindulgent.

A marsh can accommodate water whether it is clean or dirty, spring water or salt water, but there is a limit to what the marsh can hold. Your income can come from many sources, but if you spend too much your resources will dry up. Therefore it is essential to balance income and expenditure, and also to keep your character unblemished.

Line of Change

FIRST NINE

He does not go out of the courtyard outside his door. There will be no mistakes.

You feel like an inexperienced youngster arriving at work for the first time. Learn self-control. Everything will work out well.

SECOND NINE

He does not go out of the courtyard inside his gate. There will be bad fortune.

You are not working well with your colleagues. You also spurn the advice of more experienced people. Try not to let the opportunities slip by. Act when the going is good.

THIRD SIX

Tears will fall because he does not observe the restrictions. There is no fault in this.

You have only yourself to blame for your unhappiness. Everything should be all right if you change your attitude. Practise self-control.

FOURTH SIX

He accepts the limitations peacefully. There will be success.

You must be like the Prime Minister who owes his position to the fact that he treats staff kindly and knows how to control his emotions. Take on the responsibilities appropriate to your job.

FIFTH NINE

He willingly accepts the limitations. There will be good fortune. His advance is praised.

A good leader is like the Emperor. His determination will lead you to prosperity. Hc always follows a middle path.

TOP SIX

He is distressed by the limitations. Even when he acts properly there will be misfortune. Although there are regrets, they will disappear.

Life consists of good and bad times. Unhappiness is a normal part of life. Do not try to fight it.

CHUNG FU

Inner Confidence

HEXAGRAM 61

Inner confidence. Pigs and fish mean good fortune. It is helpful to cross the great river. It is helpful to behave properly.

Chung Fu combines the marsh and wind in its lower and upper hexagrams *Tui* and *Sun*. Objects obey the force of the wind: for example, marsh water ripples under a breeze. *Tui* is happiness and follows *Sun* obediently, just as a strong emperor wins the support of his people. *Chung Fu*, with confidence, honesty and loyalty, affects everyone with whom it comes into contact. This hexagram is hard on the outside and empty on the inside, like a wooden boat. Everyone in the boat has a common aim so that they can direct their work to the common good. If an emperor rules wisely he can actually reform his people; in the same way the wind which ruffles the water actually affects the creatures in the water. *Chung Fu* is based on the confidence that everything will succeed and that Heaven will correct all bad habits.

Line of Change

FIRST NINE

He is ready. There will be good fortune. Otherwise he would be uneasy.

If someone gives you the first chance to try something new, give it careful thought. Be prepared. You could be lucky.

SECOND NINE

The crane calls out from her cover. Her chicks answer back. 'I have a good cup full which I will share with you.'

Your actions should set an example to others. They can have far-reaching consequences, just as the call of a crane can be heard at great distances. Not only will you be respected but other people will want to be with you.

THIRD SIX

He meets his companions. He beats the drum and then stops. He weeps and then sings.

There is a good deal of happiness at the top of the *Tui* trigram, but be careful. Working too closely with other people can cause arguments. You may come to rely too much on their moods.

FOURTH SIX

The moon is almost full. The horse has lost his mate. There is nothing wrong in this.

The moon is almost full and your plans are nearly completed. Everything will work out well because the Fourth Six is leaving the Third Six and joining the Fifth Nine. It is good that you have decided to leave an untrustworthy friend.

FIFTH NINE

He is united with others because he is confident. There will be no mistakes.

Beware of choosing colleagues because they are your friends. Choose them for their honesty, skills and trustworthiness.

TOP NINE

The voice of the cockerel rises up to Heaven. Even if he behaves properly there is bad fortune.

Try not to be too confident. Chickens can never fly but they attempt to if you try to catch them. Although you realize that you will not be promoted you have foolishly refused to step down.

HSAIO KUO

Minor Problems

HEXAGRAM 62

Minor problems. Success. It is useful to behave properly. This is appropriate for minor things but not for more important things. The bird on the wing brings the message. It is good to come down but not to go up. There will be extremely good fortune.

Hsiao Kuo combines mountain and thunder in its lower and upper trigrams, *Ken* and *Chen*. The hexagram is weak outside but obstinate inside and is confused in its behaviour. Unless you think carefully about your actions you will probably make small mistakes but these can always be corrected. Treat everything as an experience and it will work its way through naturally if you are patient.

Since this hexagram is more yin than yang it cannot make any direct decisions and therefore makes mistakes. The thunder which rolls over the mountain's peak can be clearly heard, just as a wise man's behaviour is in the public gaze. Therefore he is modest, well mannered and reliable.

Line of Change

FIRST SIX

The bird is on the wing. There will be misfortune.

Do not be like a bird which flies higher and higher without a thought for the future. Think about what you need and how you will achieve it. You are bound to make mistakes if you rush towards a goal but forget to consider the means of achieving it.

SECOND SIX

He passes by his ancestor. He meets his grandmother. He does not do anything against his ruler. He meets his official. There will be no mistakes.

Never forget your manners. A traveller who returns home should never visit his grandmother before his grandfather. An envoy should never visit the Prime Minister before the Emperor.

THIRD NINE

Someone comes up and attacks him because he is not sufficiently careful. There will be misfortune.

You are very lucky at the moment. Try not to be too self-assured because you will make others jealous. The yin lines in this hexagram are jealous of the Third Nine's good fortune.

FOURTH NINE

There are no mistakes here. Instead of passing by he meets him. Carrying on brings danger and care should be taken. Do not always try to use proper behaviour.

It depends on your present state of mind whether you will act forcefully or be submissive. If you are too forceful you may suffer loss, but if you are too weak you may be insulted. Do not force yourself on others. Be on your guard.

FIFTH SIX

There is a heavy cloud which is coming from our lands in the west, but no rain. The prince fires and hits the bird in the cave.

Your job may be very important but you are trapped in your present position. When the sky is full of clouds it does not always rain. In the same way you may have a good deal of experience but you may never be promoted.

TOP SIX

He does not meet him but passes by. The bird on the wing has flown far away from him. There will be bad fortune. This is a sign of pain and misfortune.

Follow Heaven's way, not the way of human relationships. Curb your pride or your arrogance will separate you from other people and you will lose their respect. The holy man advises you to be considerate and fair in your judgement of others.

CHI CHI

Already Done

Already done. Minor success. It is helpful to behave properly. There will be good fortune to begin with, but chaos at the end.

Chi Chi combines fire and water in its lower and upper trigrams *Li* and *K'an*. In this hexagram the water is above the fire, and this can be achieved by boiling a pan of water or by cooking food. The steam which is produced by the hot water can be used for the general good to drive machinery, or it becomes a cloud which will eventually provide moisture for everything on earth. *K'an* represents an adult man and *Li* represents an adult woman, and although they have different functions, like fire and water, they can be successful when they join together.

The yin and yang lines are in their correct positions in the hexagram, therefore all endeavours can work harmoniously and finish successfully. When the love between a man and woman reaches its peak they decide to marry and afterwards they will be happy and calm in each other's company. A second emotional peak in their marriage occurs when they have a child. At *Chi Chi*'s highest point everything will work out successfully. Yang is obstinate on the outside and yin is weak on the inside, which is exactly how it ought to be, but since everything is at its highest point there will be a period of decline after the Fifth Nine. The yang will go up to the Top Six, a yin line, and there will be confusion.

Line of Change

FIRST NINE

He puts the brakes on his wheels. He is like a creature who has wet his tail. There will be no mistakes.

Work hard and direct your energies towards the future, particularly if you are still young. Your effort will not go unrewarded.

SECOND SIX

He is like a woman who has lost her screen. She does not go after it. She will get it back in seven days.

A determined attitude will help you finish any project on time. Do not let yourself be sidetracked by trivial matters. If a woman drops a piece of jewellery there is no point in her searching for it. Whether it is cheap or expensive, whoever picks it up will return it to her or to a police station.

THIRD NINE

The noble ancestor destroyed the devil's territory but took three years to subdue it. Lesser people should not be used.

Personal pride will make you easily susceptible to flattery. Once you succumb to flattery you cannot concentrate fully on your work.

FOURTH SIX

The best clothes are now in rags. In the end he will be careful all day.

Be careful and alert as if you were sailing in a wooden boat. If the boat begins to leak you will need a bundle of rags to prevent it from sinking. In the same way you must be prepared for all eventualities.

FIFTH NINE

His neighbour in the east kills an ox, but he does not have as much as his neighbour in the west who sacrifices. His sacrifice brings great blessings.

Virtue is an important attribute in an Emperor. He recognizes opportunities and exploits them, but he does not overestimate his ability. Be like this Emperor.

TOP SIX

His head is in the water. There is danger.

63 CHI CHI

Everything has reached its limit in this hexagram and must now go into decline. Since *K'an* is at the top of the hexagram there are dangers lying in wait for you. Do not be like a fox who avoids a trap and therefore becomes arrogant. As he turns to wash his face in the river he falls into the water. Do not become complacent just because everything is running smoothly.

WEI CHI

Not Yet Done

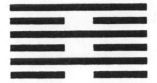

HEXAGRAM 64

Not yet done. Success. A young fox crossing the stream gets his tail wet. There is no advantage in this.

Wei Chi follows *Chi Chi* and fights for future developments. The lower and upper trigrams combine *K'an* and *Li*. Although *Li* is fire you have to work hard to arrive at that point because *K'an* is dangerous. The future depends greatly on cooperative hard work, but this can be severely set back by arrogance and prejudice. You must be alert and careful like a small fox who tries to cross a stream without wetting its tail.

Fifth Six is like a willing official who works hard and knows that everything will find its right path in time. You cannot expect everything to run perfectly and be free from mistake, like the fox who could not help dropping his tail in the water as he tried to cross the river. He may not have been successful but he learned from this experience. The yin and yang lines are not in a perfect position but they can work together towards a successful future.

Fire rises upwards and water flows downwards and since their natures are different they cannot cooperate; if they work together they should not expect immediate success.

When two people of different characters work together they must give sufficient consideration to each other. Through common characteristics such as honesty and determination they will eventually make good progress.

Line of Change

FIRST SIX

He gets his tail wet. This will cause regret.

64 WEI CHI

Carefully consider whether you are able to take on such great responsibilities. You do not want to be like a young fox who soaks his beautiful tail while trying to cross a river. Do not give others the chance to criticize you.

SECOND NINE

He puts the brakes on his wheels. Proper behaviour will bring good fortune.

You have to be like a car which keeps on going even though the road is full of potholes. Keep going forward. It is the easiest and most successful way forward for the future.

THIRD SIX

He advances and meets misfortune before things are properly finished. It is helpful to cross the great stream.

Do not push things too far. Others may think your patience and care are a sign of a weak character, but at the moment they are appropriate. Like this yin line, you do not have the strength to lead opposition against others.

FOURTH NINE

Proper conduct will bring good fortune. All regret passes away. He is shaken and invades the devil's territory. The great country rewards him for three years.

There are dangers ahead of you which can be avoided. Once they have passed, you should strike out for what you know is right. You will not regret this.

FIFTH SIX

Proper behaviour will bring good fortune. There is no cause for regret. He has the glory of the wise man and he is sincere. There will be good fortune.

Work with people who support and encourage you. A prime minister chooses brave, determined and willing workers, and so should you. You will be lucky if you can work with a team of this calibre.

TOP NINE

He is confident and celebrates with drink. There is no wrong in this. If he wets his head he will lose his confidence.

Drinking is pleasant, but you should not become too drunk because there is always work to be done. Nothing ever stops completely. Once men have arrived on the moon, they want to visit other stars. This is the principle of circular reason which underlies the Chou *I Ching*. Everything in your life and around you continues to develop. A set of seven days is naturally followed by the first day of another seven days. This movement is endless.

Appendix 1

The Ancient Chinese Text

In the following pages we reproduce the original Chinese text of the judgements on the hexagrams by King Wen and the commentaries on the lines by Tan, the Duke of Chou. In our translation these lines appear in italics. The ancient Chinese text comes from one of the main modern Chinese commentaries on the *I Ching*, Sun Tsai Shang's *Chou I Yuan I Hsin Cheng Shih* (Taiwan, 1981).

䷾

既濟，小亨，利貞，初吉終亂。

初九，曳其輪，濡其尾，无咎。

六二，婦喪其茀，勿逐，七日得。

九三，高宗伐鬼方，三年克之，小人勿用。

六四，繻有衣袽，終日戒。

九五，東鄰殺牛，不如西鄰之禴祭，實受其福。

上六，濡其首，厲。

䷿

未濟，亨。小狐汔濟，濡其尾，无攸利。

初六，濡其尾，吝。

九二，曳其輪，貞吉。

六三，未濟，征凶。利涉大川。

九四，貞吉悔亡。震用伐鬼方，三年有賞于大國。

六五，貞吉无悔。君子之光，有孚吉。

上九，有孚于飲酒，无咎。濡其首，有孚失是。

䷼

中孚，豚魚吉，利涉大川，利貞。

初九，虞吉，有它不燕。

九二，鳴鶴在陰，其子和之。我有好爵，吾與爾靡之。

六三，得敵，或鼓或罷，或泣或歌。

六四，月幾望，馬匹亡，无咎。

九五，有孚攣如，无咎。

上九，翰音登于天，貞凶。

䷽

小過，亨，利貞。可小事，不可大事。飛鳥遺之音，不宜上，宜下，大吉。

初六，飛鳥以凶。

六二，過其祖，遇其妣，不及其君，遇其臣，无咎。

九三，弗過防之，從或戕之，凶。

九四，无咎，弗過遇之，往厲，必戒。勿用永貞。

六五，密雲不雨，自我西郊，公弋取彼在穴。

上六，弗遇過之，飛鳥離之，凶，是謂災眚。

䷺

渙，亨。王假有廟，利涉大川，利貞。

初六，用拯，馬壯，吉。

九二，渙奔其機，悔亡。

六三，渙其躬，无悔。

六四，渙其羣，元吉。渙有丘，匪夷所思。

九五，渙汗其大號，渙王居，无咎。

上九，渙其血，去逖出，咎无。

䷼

節，亨。苦節不可貞。

初九，不出戶庭，无咎。

九二，不出門庭，凶。

六三，不節若，則嗟若，无咎。

六四，安節，亨。

九五，甘節，吉。往有尚。

上六，苦節，貞凶，悔亡。

䷸

巽，小亨。利有攸往，利見大人。

初六，進退，利武人之貞。

九二，巽在牀下，用史巫紛若，吉，无咎。

九三，頻巽，吝。

六四，悔亡，田獲三品。

九五，貞吉，悔亡。无不利。无始有終。先庚三日，後庚三日，吉。

上九，巽在牀下，喪其資斧，貞凶。

䷹

兌，亨，利貞。

初九，和兌，吉。

九二，孚兌，吉。悔亡。

六三，來兌，凶。

九四，商兌未寧，介疾有喜。

九五，孚于剝，有厲。

上六，引兌。

豐，亨。王假之，勿憂；宜日中。

初九，遇其配主，雖旬无咎，往有尚。

六二，豐其蔀，日中見斗。往得疑疾，有孚發若，吉。

九三，豐其沛，日中見沫，折其右肱，无咎。

九四，豐其蔀，日中見斗，遇其夷主，吉。

六五，來章，有慶，譽，吉。

上六，豐其屋，蔀其家，闚其戶，闃其无人，三歲不覿，凶。

旅，小亨，旅貞吉。

初六，旅瑣瑣，斯其所取災。

六二，旅即次，懷其資，得童僕貞。

九三，旅焚其次，喪其童僕，貞厲。

九四，旅于處，得其資斧，我心不快。

六五，射雉，一矢亡。終以譽命。

上九，鳥焚其巢，旅人先笑後號咷。喪牛于易，凶。

漸，女歸，吉；利貞。

初六，鴻漸于干，小子厲，有言无咎。

六二，鴻漸于磐，飲食衎衎，吉。

九三，鴻漸于陸。夫征不復，婦孕不育，凶。利禦寇。

六四，鴻漸于木，或得其桷，无咎。

九五，鴻漸于陵，婦三歲不孕，終莫之勝，吉。

上九，鴻漸于陸，其羽可用爲儀，吉。

歸妹，征凶，无攸利。

初九，歸妹以娣，跛能履，征吉。

九二，眇其視，利幽人之貞。

六三，歸妹以須，反歸以娣。

九四，歸妹愆期，遲歸有時。

六五，帝乙歸妹，其君之袂不如其娣之袂，良。月幾望，吉。

上六，女承筐，无實，士刲羊，无血，无攸利。

震，亨。震來虩虩，笑言啞啞，震驚百里，不喪匕鬯。

初九，震來虩虩，後笑言啞啞，吉。

六二，震來厲，億喪貝，躋于九陵，勿逐，七日得。

六三，震蘇蘇，震行无眚。

九四，震遂泥。

六五，震往來厲。意无喪，有事。

上六，震索索，視矍矍，征凶。震不于其躬，于其鄰，无咎。婚媾有言。

艮其背，不獲其身；行其庭，不見其人，无咎。

初六，艮其趾，无咎。利永貞。

六二，艮其腓，不拯其隨，其心不快。

九三，艮其限，列其夤，厲薰心。

六四，艮其身，无咎。

六五，艮其輔，言有序，悔亡。

上九，敦艮，吉。

䷰

革，己日乃孚，元亨利貞，悔亡。

初九，鞏用黃牛之革。

六二，己日乃革之，征吉无咎。

九三，征凶，貞厲。革言三就，有孚。

九四，悔亡，有孚改命，吉。

九五，大人虎變，未占有孚。

上六，君子豹變，小人革面，征凶，居貞吉。

䷱

鼎，元吉，亨。

初六，鼎顛趾，利出否。得妾以其子，无咎。

九二，鼎有實，我仇有疾，我不能，即吉。

九三，鼎耳革，其行塞。雉膏不食，方雨虧悔，終吉。

九四，鼎折足，覆公餗，其形渥，凶。

六五，鼎，黃耳金鉉，利貞。

上九，鼎玉鉉，大吉；无不利。

䷮

困，亨，貞，大人吉，无咎。有言不信。

初六，臀困于株木，入于幽谷，三歲不覿。

九二，困于酒食，朱紱方來，利用享祀，征凶，无咎。

六三，困于石，據于蒺藜。入于其宮，不見其妻，凶。

九四，來徐徐，困于金車，吝，有終。

九五，劓刖，困于赤紱，乃徐有說，利用祭祀。

上六，困于葛藟，于臲卼，曰動悔，有悔，征吉。

䷯

井，改邑不改井，无喪无得；往來井井。汔至，亦未繘井，羸其瓶，凶。

初六，井泥不食，舊井无禽。

九二，井谷射鮒，甕敝漏。

九三，井渫不食，爲我心惻，可用汲。王明，並受其福。

六四，井甃无咎。

九五，井冽，寒泉食。

上六，井收勿幕，有孚元吉。

䷬

萃，亨。王假有廟，利見大人，亨，利貞。用大牲吉。利有攸往。

初六，有孚不終，乃亂乃萃，若號，一握爲笑，勿恤，往无咎。

六二，引吉，无咎。孚乃利用禴。

六三，萃如。嗟如。无攸利，往无咎，小吝。

九四，大吉，无咎。

九五，萃有位，无咎。匪孚，元永貞，悔亡。

上六，齎咨，涕洟，无咎。

䷭

升，元亨，用見大人。勿恤，南征吉。

初六，允升，大吉。

九二，孚乃利用禴，无咎。

九三，升虛邑。

六四，王用亨于岐山，吉无咎。

六五，貞吉，升階。

上六，冥升，升于不息之貞。

四三

夬，揚于王庭，孚號，有厲。告自邑，不利即戎，利有攸往。

初九，壯于前趾，往不勝，爲咎。

九二，惕號，莫夜有戎，勿恤。

九三，壯于頄，有凶。君子夬夬，獨行遇雨，若濡有慍，无咎。

九四，臀无膚，其行次且，牽羊悔亡，聞言不信。

九五，莧陸，夬夬，中行无咎。

上六，无號，終有凶。

四四

姤，女壯，勿用取女。

初六，繫于金柅，貞吉。有攸往，見凶。羸豕孚蹢躅。

九二，包有魚，无咎；不利賓。

九三，臀无膚，其行次且，厲；无大咎也。

九四，包无魚，起凶。

九五，以杞包瓜，含章；有隕自天。

上九，姤其角，吝，无咎。

損，有孚元吉，无咎，可貞。利有攸往。曷之用？二簋可用享。

初九，已事遄往，无咎，酌損之。

九二，利貞，征凶。弗損益之。

六三，三人行，則損一人；一人行，則得其友。

六四，損其疾，使遄有喜，无咎。

六五，或益之。十朋之龜，弗克違；元吉。

上九，弗損，益之，无咎，貞吉。利有攸往，得臣无家。

益，利有攸往，利涉大川。

初九，利用為大作。元吉，无咎。

六二，或益之十朋之龜，弗克違，永貞吉。王用亨于帝，吉。

六三，益之用，凶事，无咎。有孚中行，告公用圭。

六四，中行告，公從，利用為依，遷國。

九五，有孚惠心，勿問元吉。有孚惠我德。

上九，莫益之，或擊之，立心勿恆，凶。

䷦

蹇，利西南，不利東北；利見大人，貞吉。

初六，往蹇，來譽。

六二，王臣蹇蹇，匪躬之故。

九三，往蹇來反。

六四，往蹇來連。

九五，大蹇朋來。

上六，往蹇，來碩，吉；利見大人。

䷧

解，利西南，无所往，其來復吉。有攸往，夙吉。

初六，无咎。

九二，田獲三狐，得黃矢，貞吉。

六三，負且乘，致寇至；貞吝。

九四，解而拇，朋至斯孚。

六五，君子維，有解，吉。有孚于小人。

上六，公用射隼，于高墉之上，獲之无不利。

家人，利女貞。

初九，閑有家，悔亡。

六二，无攸遂，在中饋，貞吉。

九三，家人嗃嗃，悔，厲吉。婦子嘻嘻，終吝。

六四，富家大吉。

九五，王假有家，勿恤，吉。

上九，有孚，威如，終吉。

睽，小事吉。

初九，悔亡，喪馬勿逐自復，見惡人无咎。

九二，遇主于巷，无咎。

六三，見輿曳，其牛掣，其人天且劓。无初有終。

九四，睽孤，遇元夫交孚，厲，无咎。

六五，悔亡，厥宗噬膚，往何咎。

上九，睽孤，見豕負塗，載鬼一車，先張之弧，後說之弧；匪寇，婚媾。往遇雨則吉。

晉☰☰

晉。康侯用錫馬蕃庶，晝日三接。

初六，晉如摧如，貞吉；罔孚裕，无咎。

六二，晉如愁如，貞吉；受茲介福于王母。

六三，眾允悔亡。

九四，晉如鼫鼠，貞厲。

六五，悔亡，失得勿恤，往吉，无不利。

上九，晉其角，維用伐邑，厲吉；无咎；貞吝。

明夷☰☰

明夷，利艱貞。

初九，明夷于飛，垂其翼。君子于行，三日不食。有攸往，主人有言。

六二，明夷，夷于左股；用拯，馬壯吉。

九三，明夷于南狩，得其大首；不可疾，貞。

六四，入于左腹，有獲明夷之心·于出門庭。

六五，箕子之明夷，利貞。

上六，不明晦，初登于天，後入于地。

䷠

遯，亨；小，利貞。

初六，遯尾，厲。勿用有攸往。

六二，執之用黃牛之革，莫之勝說。

九三，係遯，有疾厲。畜臣妾吉。

九四，好遯，君子言；小人否。

九五，嘉遯，貞吉。

上九，飛遯，无不利。

䷡

大壯，利貞。

初九，壯于趾，征凶；有孚。

九二，貞吉。

九三，小人用壯，君子用罔，貞厲。羝羊觸藩，羸其角。

九四，貞吉悔亡。藩決不羸，壯于大輿之輹。

六五，喪羊于易，无悔。

上六，羝羊觸藩，不能退，不能遂。无攸利，艱則吉

☷☶

咸，亨。利貞，取女吉。

初六，咸其拇。

六二，咸其腓，凶，居吉。

九三，咸其股，執其隨，往吝。

九四，貞吉，悔亡，憧憧往來，朋從爾思。

九五，咸其脢，无悔。

上六，咸其輔頰舌。

☳☴

恆，亨，无咎，利貞。利有攸往。

初六，浚恆，貞凶；无攸利。

九二，悔亡。

九三，不恆其德，或承之羞，貞吝。

九四，田无禽。

六五，恆其德，貞；婦人吉，夫子凶。

上六，振恆凶。

䷜

習坎，有孚。維心亨，行有尚。

初六，習坎，入于坎窞，凶。

九二，坎有險，求小得。

六三，來之坎坎，險且枕，入于坎窞，勿用。

六四，樽酒簋貳，用缶。納約自牖，終无咎。

九五，坎不盈，祗既平，无咎。

上六，係用徽纆，寘于叢棘，三歲不得，凶。

䷝

離，利貞亨。畜牝牛，吉。

初九，履錯然，敬之，无咎。

六二，黃離，元吉。

九三，日昃之離，不鼓缶而歌，則大耋之嗟，凶。

九四，突如其來如、焚如、死如、棄如。

六五，出涕沱若，戚嗟若。吉。

上九，王用出征，有嘉折首，獲匪其醜。无咎。

䷚

頤，貞吉。觀頤，自求口實。

初九，舍爾靈龜，觀我朵頤，凶。

六二，顛頤拂經，于邱頤，征凶。

六三，拂頤，貞凶。十年勿用，無攸利。

六四，顛頤吉。虎視眈眈，其欲逐逐。無咎。

六五，拂經，居貞吉。不可涉大川。

上九，由頤厲吉，利涉大川。

䷛

大過，棟橈。利有攸往，亨。

初六，藉用白茅，無咎。

九二，枯楊生稊，老夫得女妻，無不利。

九三，棟橈，凶。

九四，棟隆，吉。有它吝。

九五，枯楊生華，老婦得其士夫，無咎無譽。

上六，過涉滅頂，凶。無咎。

二五

无妄，元亨利貞。其匪正有眚，不利有攸往。

初九，无妄往吉。

六二，不耕穫，不菑畬，則利有攸往。

六三，无妄之災，或繫之牛。行人得之，邑人之災。

九四，可貞，无咎。

九五，无妄之疾，勿藥有喜。

上九，无妄行有眚，无攸利。

二六

大畜，利貞，不家食吉，利涉大川。

初九，有厲利巳。

九二，輿說輹。

九三，良馬逐，利艱貞。日閑輿衛，利有攸往。

六四，童牛之牿，元吉。

六五，豶豕之牙，吉。

上九，向天之衢，亨。

䷖

剝，不利有攸往。

初六，剝牀以足，蔑貞。凶。

六二，剝牀以辨，蔑貞。凶。

六三，剝之，无咎。

六四，剝牀以膚，凶。

六五，貫魚，以宮人寵。无不利。

上九，碩果不食，君子得輿，小人剝廬。

䷗

復，亨。出入无疾，朋來无咎。反復其道，七日來復，利有攸往。

初九，不遠復，无祗悔。元吉。

六二，休復，吉。

六三，頻復，厲，无咎。

六四，中行獨復。

六五，敦復，无悔。

上六，迷復，凶。有災眚，用行師，終有大敗，以其國君凶。至于十年不克征。

噬嗑，亨。利用獄。

初九，履校滅趾，无咎。

六二，噬膚滅鼻，无咎。

六三，噬腊肉，遇毒，小吝，无咎。

九四，噬乾胏，得金矢，利艱貞吉。

六五，噬乾肉，得黃金，貞厲无咎。

上九，何校滅耳，凶。

賁，亨，小利有攸往。

初九，賁其趾，舍車而徒。

六二，賁其須。

九三，賁如濡如，永貞吉。

六四，賁如皤如，白馬翰如，匪寇婚媾。

六五，賁于丘園，束帛戔戔，吝，終吉。

上九，白賁，无咎。

䷒

臨，元亨利貞，至於八月有凶。

初九；咸臨貞吉。

九二，咸臨吉，无不利。

六三，甘臨，无攸利，旣憂之，无咎。

六四，至臨，无咎。

六五，知臨，大君之宜，吉。

上六，敦臨，吉无咎。

䷓

觀，盥而不薦，有孚顒若。

初六，童觀，小人无咎，君子客。

六二，闚觀，利女貞。

六三，觀我生進退。

六四，觀國之光，利用賓于王。

九五，觀我生，君子无咎。

上九，觀其生，君子无咎。

隨，元亨利貞，无咎。

初九，官有渝，貞吉。出門交有功。

六二，係小子，失丈夫。

六三，係丈夫，失小子。隨有求得，利居貞。

九四，隨有獲，貞凶。有孚在道，以明，何咎。

九五，孚于嘉，吉。

上六，拘係之，乃從維之，王用亨于西山。

蠱，元亨，利涉大川，先甲三日，後甲三日。

初六，幹父之蠱，有子，考无咎。厲終吉。

九二，幹母之蠱，不可貞。

九三，幹父之蠱，小有悔，无大咎。

六四，裕父之蠱，往見吝。

六五，幹父之蠱，用譽。

上九，不事王侯，高尚其事。

䷠ 謙，亨。君子有終。

初六，謙謙君子，用涉大川，吉。

六二，鳴謙貞吉。

九三，勞謙，君子有終，吉。

六四，无不利撝謙。

六五，不富以其鄰，利用侵伐，无不利。

上六，鳴謙，利用行師，征邑國。

䷏ 豫，利建侯，行師。

初六，鳴豫凶。

六二，介于石，不終日，貞吉。

六三，肝豫，悔。遲有悔。

九四，由豫，大有德，勿疑，朋盍簪。

六五，貞疾，恆不死。

上六，冥豫成，有渝，无咎。

☰☰

同人于野，亨。利涉大川，利君子貞。

初九，同人于門，无咎。

六二，同人于宗，吝。

九三，伏戎于莽，升其高陵，三歲不興。

九四，乘其墉，弗攻克，吉。

九五，同人先號咷而後笑，大師克相遇。

上九，同人于郊，无悔。

☰☰

大有，元亨。

初九，无交害，匪咎。艱則无咎。

九二，大車以載，有攸往，无咎。

九三，公用亨于天子，小人弗克。

九四，匪其彭，无咎。

六五，厥孚交如，威如，吉。

上九，自天祐之，吉无不利。

▉▉ 泰

泰，小往大來，吉亨。

初九，拔茅茹，以其彙，征吉。

九二，包荒，用馮河，不遐遺，朋亡，得尚于中行。

九三，无平不陂，无往不復，艱貞无咎。勿恤其孚，于食有福。

六四，翩翩，不富以其鄰，不戒以孚。

六五，帝乙歸妹，以祉元吉。

上六，城復于隍，勿用師，自邑告命，貞吝。

▉▉ 否

否之匪人，不利君子貞。大往小來。

初六，拔茅茹，以其彙，貞吉亨。

六二，包承，小人吉。大人否亨。

六三，包羞。

九四，有命无咎，疇離祉。

九五，休否，大人吉。其亡其亡，繫於包桑。

上九，傾否，先否後吉。

䷈

小畜，亨。密雲不雨，自我西郊。

初九，復自道，何其咎，吉。

九二，牽復，吉。

九三，輿說輻，夫妻反目。

六四，有孚，血去惕出，无咎。

九五，有孚攣如，富以其鄰。

上九，既雨既處，尚德，載婦貞，厲；月幾望，君子征凶。

䷉

履虎尾，不咥人，亨。

初九，素履，往，无咎。

九二，履道坦坦，幽人貞吉。

六三，眇能視，跛能履，履虎尾咥人，凶。武人爲于大君。

九四，履虎尾，愬愬終吉。

九五，夬履貞厲。

上九，視履考祥，其旋元吉。

師，貞，丈人吉，无咎。

初六，師出以律，否臧凶。

九二，在師中吉，无咎。王三錫命。

六三，師或輿尸，凶。

六四，師左次，无咎。

六五，田有禽，利執言，无咎。長子帥師。弟子輿尸，貞凶。

上六，大君有命，開國承家，小人勿用。

比，吉。原筮，元永貞，无咎。不寧方來，後夫凶。

初六，有孚，比之无咎。有孚盈缶，終來有他吉。

六二，比之自內，貞吉。

六三，比之匪人。

六四，外比之，貞吉。

九五，顯比。王用三驅失前禽。邑人不誡，吉。

上六，比之无首，凶。

需 ䷄

需，有孚，光亨，貞吉。利涉大川。

初九，需于郊，利用恆，无咎。

九二，需于沙，小有言，終吉。

九三，需于泥，致寇至。

六四，需于血，出自穴。

九五，需于酒食，貞吉。

上六，入于穴，有不速之客三人來。敬之終吉。

訟 ䷅

訟，有孚，**窒**，惕，中吉，終凶。利見大人，不利涉大川。

初六，不永所事，小有言，終吉。

九二，不克訟，歸而逋，其邑人三百戶，无眚。

六三，食舊德，貞厲，終吉。或從王事，无成。

九四，不克訟，復即命、渝，安貞吉。

九五，訟，元吉。

上九，或錫之鞶帶，終朝三褫之。

☲☷

屯，元亨利貞。勿用有攸往。利建侯。

初九，盤桓，利居貞，利建侯。

六二，屯如邅如，乘馬班如，匪寇婚媾。女子貞不字，十年乃字。

六三，卽鹿无虞，惟入于林中。君子幾不如舍，往吝。

六四，乘馬班如，求婚媾，往吉，无不利。

九五，屯其膏，小貞吉，大貞凶。

上六，乘馬班如，泣血漣如。

☶☵

蒙，亨。匪我求蒙童，蒙童求我。初筮告，再三瀆，瀆則不告，利貞。

初六，發蒙。利用刑人，用說桎梏，以往吝。

九二，包蒙，吉。納婦，吉，子克家。

六三，勿用取女。見金夫，不有躬，无攸利。

九四，困蒙，吝。

六五，童蒙，吉。

上九，擊蒙，不利爲寇，利禦寇。

☰☰☰

乾，元亨利貞。

初九，潛龍勿用。

九二，見龍在田，利見大人。

九三，君子終日乾乾，夕惕若厲，无咎。

九四，或躍在淵，无咎。

九五，飛龍在天，利見大人。

上九，亢龍有悔。

☷☷☷

坤，元亨利牝馬之貞。君子有攸往，先迷後得，主利。西南得朋，東北喪朋，安貞，吉。

初六，履霜堅冰至。

六二，直方大，不習，无不利。

六三，含章可貞，或從王事，无成有終。

六四，**括囊无咎、无譽。**

六五，黃裳元吉。

上六，龍戰于野，其血玄黃。

Appendix 2

For those wishing to use the three coin method described on pp. 38/39, we append below the key for identifying the hexagrams.

TRIGRAMS UPPER LOWER	Ch'ien	Chen	K'an	Ken	K'un	Sun	Li	Tui
Chien	1	34	5	26	11	9	14	43
Chen	25	51	3	27	24	42	21	17
K'an	6	40	29	4	7	59	64	47
Ken	33	62	39	52	15	53	56	31
K'un	12	16	8	23	2	20	35	45
Sun	44	32	48	18	46	57	50	28
Li	13	55	63	22	36	37	30	49
Tui	10	54	60	41	19	61	38	58

Notes

CHAPTER 1

1. In Theodore de Bary (ed.), *Sources of Chinese Tradition*, 2 vols., Columbia University Press, 1960, vol. I, p. 197.
2. See Martin Palmer (ed.) *T'ung Shu: The Ancient Chinese Almanac*, Rider, 1986, p. 15.
3. See Kwang-chih Chang, *Shang Civilization*, Yale University Press, 1980, pp. 34 ff.; Robert Temple, *Conversations with Eternity*, Rider, 1984.
4. See *She King*, trans. James Legge, *The Chinese Classics*, Oxford University Press, 1871; Southern Materials Center, Taipai, 1983, vol. IV, p. 437.
5. *Li Ki*, trans. James Legge, *The Sacred Books of the East*, Oxford University Press, 1855, vol. XVIII, pp. 349–50.
6. Hellmut Wilhelm, *Change: Eight Lectures on the I Ching*, Routledge & Kegan Paul, 1961, p. 11.
7. *Kwun Yum Fortune*, Tung Wah Group of Hospitals, Hong Kong, 1983, p. 105.
8. *Predictions of Wong Tai Sin*, Tung Wah Group of Hospitals, Hong Kong, 1984, p. 105.
9. Confucius, *The Analects*, trans. D. C. Lau, Penguin Books, 1979, p. 107.
10. *Selections from the Records of the Historian Ssu-ma Ch'ien*, trans. Yang Hsien-yi and Gladys Yang, Peking, 1979, p. 178.
11. Palmer, op. cit., p. 18.
12. See Kwok Man Ho, Martin Palmer and Joanne O'Brien, *Lines of Destiny*, Rider, 1986.
13. Quoted in Kenneth J. DeWoskin, *Doctors, Diviners and Magicians of Ancient China*, Columbia University Press, 1983, p. 112.
14. Quoted in Arthur F. Wright (ed.), *The Confucian Persuasion*, Stanford University Press, 1960, p. 119.
15. *Alchemy, Medicine and Religion: The Nei P'ien of Ko Hung*, trans. J. R. Ware, MIT Press, 1966, p. 147.
16. See Joseph Needham, *Sience and Civilization in China*, Cambridge University Press, 1956, vol. II, p. 333.
17. Michael Saso, *The Teachings of Taoist Master Chuang*, Yale University Press, 1978, p. 8.

CHAPTER 2

1. Immanuel C. Y. Hsu, *The Rise of Modern China*, Oxford University Press, 1975, p. 36.
2. See also Chan Siu-wai, *Buddhism in Late Ching Political Thought*, Chinese University Press, Hong Kong, 1985.
3. See, for example, Jonathan Spence, *Emperor of China*, Penguin Books, 1977, pp. 44–6.
4. Louis Le Comte SJ, *Journey Through the Empire of China*, Tooke, 3rd edn, 1699, p. 191.
5. *Yi King*, trans. James Legge, *The Sacred Books of the East*, Oxford University Press, 1882, vol. XVI.
6. *The I Ching or the Book of Changes*, trans. into German by Richard Wilhelm and rendered into English by Cary F. Baynes, 2 vols., Routledge & Kegan Paul, 1951.
7. See, for example, the chapter on Christian mission in Richard Wilhelm's *The Soul of China*, Cape, 1928.
8. See W. E. Soothill, *The Three Religions of China*, Hodder & Stoughton, 1912, pp. 125–7. For a more recent version of the same idea see D. Howard Smith, *Chinese Religion*, Weidenfeld & Nicolson, 1968.
9. Timothy Richards, *The New Testament of Higher Buddhism*, T. & T. Clark, Edinburgh, 1910, ch. 1.
10. *The I Ching or Book of Changes*, trans. Wilhelm, p. xlv.
11. Aisin Gioro Pu Yi, *From Emperor to Citizen*, Foreign Languages Press, Peking, 1979, especially vol. I.
12. See, for example, Reginald F. Johnson, *Twilight in the Forbidden City*, Gollancz, 1934; Oxford University Press, Hong Kong, 1985.
13. Alfred Douglas, *The Oracle of Change*, Gollancz, 1971.
14. John Blofeld, *I Ching*, Allen & Unwin, 1964.

CHAPTER 3

1. *Yi King*, trans. James Legge, op. cit., pp. 369–70, para. 61.
2. See chapter 2, notes 13 and 14 above.
3. *The I Ching or Book of Changes*, trans. Wilhelm, p. 724.
4. Palmer, op. cit.

CHAPTER 4

1. See Kwok Man Ho, Palmer and O'Brien, op. cit.
2. Lo Kuan-chung, *San Kuo Chih Yen-I*, trans. as *Romance of the Three Kingdoms* by C. H. Prewitt-Taylor, Tuttle, Japan, 1959, pp. 1 and 623.
3. See Hellmut Wilhelm, op. cit., pp. 25 ff.
4. *Chuan Commentary*, Book X, Year 25; trans. James Legge, *The Chinese Classics*, Oxford University Press, 1871, vol V, p. 708.
5. Quoted in Needham, op. cit.

ABOUT THE AUTHORS

Kwok Man Ho is a practising Chinese astrologer and head of the Chinese section of the International Consultancy on Religion, Education and Culture (ICOREC). Martin Palmer, a graduate of Cambridge with a degree in Theology and Religious Studies, is a student of Chinese and the director of ICOREC. Joanne O'Brien holds an MA in theology and is a member of the ICOREC team. All three live in Manchester.